*Life as a Pilgrimage*

# Life as a Pilgrimage

## Faith, Economics and Social Justice

Charles K. Wilber

University of Notre Dame

Life as a Plgrimage
Faith, Economics and Social Justice

ISBN 978-1-7352702-3-4

Cover Design by: Jane Pitz

Published by
**CORBY BOOKS**
P.O. Box 93
Notre Dame, IN 46556
corbybooks.com

Manufactured in the United States of America

# Ultreïa

With this book I salute, *Ultreïa*, my many companions on the way, onwards and upwards my friends.

The word Ultreïa comes from the Latin meaning 'beyond'. Ultreïa is a salute made by one pilgrim to another as they pass on the Camino de Santiago de Compostela. It not only means have a good journey, but goes deeper, encouraging you to keep on going beyond what you think you can, always heading onwards.

It is believed that Medieval pilgrims used to greet each other with Ultreïa. The word is mentioned in the Codex Calixtinus (the first Camino de Santiago guide! dating back to the 12th century), from the Song of Ultreïa, a song for pilgrims on their way to Santiago. (See http://www.pilgrimroads.com/2010/12/ultreia/)

## Ultreïa

Every morning we take the Camino,
Every morning we go farther,
Day after day the route calls us,
It's the voice of [Santiago de] Compostela!

Chorus:
Onward! Onward! And upward!
God assist us!

Way of earth and way of faith,
Ancient road of Europe,
The Milky Way of Charlemagne,
It's the Chemin of all the Santiago pilgrims!

And over there at the end of the continent,
Santiago waits for us,
His smile always fixed
On the sun that dies at Finisterre.

# Dedication

*The growing good of the world is partly dependent on unhistoric acts;*
*and that things are not so ill with you and me as they might have*
*been, is half owing to the number who lived faithfully a hidden life,*
*and rest in unvisited tombs.*

— George Eliot, *Middlemarch*

This memoir is dedicated to that "great cloud of witnesses" (Heb 12:1), named and un-named, that I crossed paths with during my journey these past many years. They have been my companions on the Way. The example of their lives has been like the salute, Ultreia, Ever Onwards. My life has been shaped by their influence. In particular, I must credit the Congregation of Holy Cross and its spiritual direction as pivotal in my formation. It was at the University of Portland where I first became exposed to the spiritual and cultural riches of Catholicism. It is at the University of Notre Dame for the past 45 years that I have come to embrace the motto of the Congregation: Ave Crux, Spes Unica, "Hail the Cross, Our Only Hope."

I owe deep gratitude to Jim Langford, publisher of Corby Publishing, not only for agreeing to publish my memoir, but also for his advice and direction throughout the process. I want to thank my dear friend of 45 years and companion on the Way, Jane Pitz, for her design work on the cover.

Finally, I must recognize and thank the most important witness and companion on the Way, my wife and partner of many years, Mary Ellen Wilber; both for her steadfast support and for her participation in the Catholic Action activities that have shaped our lives.

# Table of Contents

# CHAPTER I

## On Pilgrimage

### The Road Ahead

*"MY LORD GOD, I have no idea where I am going.*
*I do not see the road ahead of me.*
*I cannot know for certain where it will end.*
*Nor do I really know myself, and the fact that I think that I am following*
*your will does not mean that I am actually doing so.*
*But I believe that the desire to please you does in fact please you.*
*And I hope I have that desire in all that I am doing.*
*I hope that I will never do anything apart from that desire.*
*And I know that if I do this you will lead me by the right road though*
*I may know nothing about it.*
*Therefore, will I trust you always though I may seem to be lost*
*and in the shadow of death.*
*I will not fear, for you are ever with me, and you will never leave me*
*to face my perils alone."*

—THOMAS MERTON

WHY WOULD AN ORDINARY PERSON, one who had not done anything that the wider world found exceptional, write a memoir and why would anyone want to read such a memoir? Good questions! In my case my good friend, Michael Baxter, kept at me to do so. He finally convinced me that the story of my life's journey attempting, however fitfully, to follow Jesus provides

1

lessons for others who are on the same journey. In my case, Catholic social thought (CST) was and is my guide .

My life has coincided with much of recent American history. I was born during the Great Depression of the 1930s; grew up during World War II and the Korean War; was married during the "heady" days of the 1950s; taught in Washington, D.C. during the hectic 1960s with the Vietnam War, civil rights battles, and the drug scene; and since the 1980s have seen the restoration of free market economics under President Reagan, the hollowing-out of American industry, the Great Recession of 2008, and in 2020 the Coronavirus pandemic that threatens to badly impact not only the economy but the very structure of our society.

Everyone's life is a journey, even if it is only from birth to death. For many of us there are detours, blind alleys, new starts, and unintended outcomes. A journey becomes a pilgrimage when there is a goal, conscious or unconscious, driving your life. In my early years I knew something was missing in my life but did not know what it was. Later, as I became aware of God's call to serve him and his people, my journey became a pilgrimage. I strayed from that path many times, from sloth, ambition, greed, and the other deadly sins. Pilgrims are sinners who pick themselves up and try again. We are never alone on that journey we call a pilgrimage: "… since we are surrounded by so great a cloud of witnesses, let us also lay aside every weight and the sin that clings so closely, and let us run with perseverance the race that is set before us, looking to Jesus the pioneer and perfecter of our faith..." (Heb 12: 1-2)

To be a witness does not mean you need be pious or heroic or extraordinary in any way but, rather, living amidst the distractions of everyday life you embrace God's love and reflect it back to all those you encounter along the way.  I owe that "great cloud of witnesses", my companions on the Way, credit for providing the examples I needed to keep the journey a pilgrimage. You will meet them as the story unfolds: my Aunt Lorena, Fr. Louie Putz, Ivan Illich, Pat & Patty Crowley, Jim Langford, Keith Egan, Rashied Omar, and many more. This memoir is about these companions as much as it is about my journey. Without them it would never have been a pilgrimage. About half of the book is devoted to them.

As a Roman Catholic, I have turned also to the saints as witnesses and mentors during my pilgrimage through life.[1] St. Benedict and his Rule have been important in my prayer life. St. Francis and his dedication to the poor helped lead me into the study of economic development.[2] St. Thomas and his Summa Theologica provided me with my introduction to both philosophy and theology.[3] St. Teresa of Calcutta[4] (better known as Mother Teresa) led me to see the individual person, not just the economy, when devising development plans.

I focus on the journey that led me from a search for meaning in life to an activist faith through a formal economics training to finally seeking a rapprochement between my faith as expressed in CST and what is known as social economics. I also write as a husband and father of seven children and I hope my experiences are useful to all Christians; and, of course, not only Christians, but all those of whatever faith who believe that their faith is important not only in their personal lives but, also in their work.

I realize that others who are also dedicated Christians, Catholics, and Protestants alike, have arrived at very different destinations than I have. My faith has led me to be a critic of our market economy and of the standard economic theory used to defend it. One of my tasks here is to show how and why my journey took the course it did.

My journey begins in the small town of The Dalles, Oregon where I was born in the depths of the Great Depression. My Dad, a carpenter, was unemployed and we moved around the Northwest picking crops in season. With the beginning of World War II my Dad got a job in the big city of Portland and it was there that I grew up and eventually met Mary Ellen Simmons, my wife and best friend of 65 years.

Christianity and concern with justice came first, economics later. After undergraduate school we spent a short time in California for work and returned to Portland and soon became involved in the Christian Family Movement (CFM). It was then that our Christian faith became revitalized as we came to realize through study of the bible and CST that we all are called to do God's work in this world. To love God is to love our neighbor.

The tradition of CST is rooted in a commitment to certain fundamental values—the right to human dignity, the need for human freedom and participation, the importance of community, and the nature of the common good. These values are drawn from the belief that each person is called to be a co-creator with God, participating in the redemption of the world and the furthering of the Kingdom. This requires social and human development where the religious and temporal aspects of life are not separated and opposed to each other.

As a result of these fundamental values two principles permeate CST. The first is a special concern for the poor and powerless which leads to a criticism of political and economic structures that oppress them. The second is a concern for certain human rights against the collectivist tendencies of the state and the neglect of the free market.

It is here that my hunger for the journey as a pilgrimage became heightened. That in turn led to our going to Puerto

Rico to teach at the Catholic University in Ponce. Working with then Msgr. Ivan Illich led me back to graduate school for my PhD. He said no one will listen unless you do.

Graduate school at the University of Maryland opened up a new world of both traditional economics and heterodox approaches such as Institutionalism and Marxism as ways of understanding poverty and issues of development for the so-called Third World.

Both in Maryland and later moving to the District of Columbia we became involved in the issues of the 1960s-- civil rights and the Vietnam War. We were active in the Catholic Interracial Council in Maryland and CFM in Washington. Teaching at The American University for 11 years I had to deal with student revolts against the Vietnam War.

In 1975 I was offered the job as Chair and Professor of Economics at the University of Notre Dame. For the past 45 years this is where our journey has unfolded. We helped found a Catholic Worker house, participated in several small Christian communities, worked to build an economics program that focused on Catholic Social Thought, and I worked as an adviser to the U.S. Catholic bishops in the writing of the pastoral letter, Economic Justice for All.

Many have been on the same journey from the church of the 1950s through the turmoil generated by Vatican II and the political and social upheavals of the 1960s into the fractured world of the 21st century. What I add are the details of one life making that journey as seen through my interactions with the many "witnesses" I encountered along the way.

This story of my life is of necessity part and parcel of the life of my family. My wife, Mary Ellen, and our seven children, Kenny, Teresa, Matt, Alice, Mary, Angie, and Louie made this journey possible. Their love and support were always there in good times and bad. The story of my intellectual and faith journey would not be complete without situating it within my family life.

Our journey together has spanned momentous times— Vietnam, the civil rights movement, the sexual revolution, Feminism, drugs, domestic and foreign terrorism. In 1970, while living in Washington, D.C., our CFM group's national program was entitled Family Revolution. Our program book that we used every two weeks, had emblazoned across the cover the words, "People Born Too Late to Live the Life for Which They Were Conditioned." This summed up many of the struggles that our family and those of many others faced, particularly during the 1960s and 1970s.

At the end of the book, after Chapter 9, I have added a section of appendices about the many "witnesses" that have influenced and directed my journey. But here I want to say something about the most important "witness" and influence in and on my journey, my wife, Mary Ellen Wilber. She has always ducked the limelight, but she deserves to be seen as the first and most important influence in our journey through life as a pilgrimage.

First of all, of course, she is the mother of our seven children and that is a task in and of itself. And while doing that:

> * She moved 14 times in 7 years including taking 4 of the children—Kenny, 4 years; Teresa, 3 years; Matt, 2 years; Alice, two weeks old-- to Puerto Rico by herself on a series of flights that took almost 24 hours.
>
> * She co-chaired the Catholic Interracial Council in Prince Georges County Maryland in 1963-67 at a time when that was a hot issue.
>
> * She housed an additional 10 people, the Furth's, for three weeks after their house burned. This was just two weeks after we moved in and I was in London for part of it.

* She took in a teenage girl, Mary Jane, for three months who was having trouble at home. The parish asked and she said yes.

* She took in 7 children of the Walshe family after their parents were taken to jail. Then after two months she helped place all but Frankie who stayed with us for two years.

* She took in one of Alice's girlfriends for six months until she graduated from high school.

* She was one of the founders of the Holy Family Catholic Worker House in South Bend and served on the board for 10 years as treasurer.

* She volunteered at the Center for the Homeless for 7 years. She volunteered at the Monroe Park Grocery Co-op for several years.

* She delivered Meals-on-Wheels every Thursday until the Coronavirus pandemic required us to self-quarantine.

Her sanity was maintained by gardening her acre plot of land. Her flowers brought loveliness into our home and she was famous for giving starts to whomever wanted some. It was here, in nature, where she felt closest to God.

And, of course, during all of this she cooked, cleaned, washed clothes, sewed, treated bumps and bruises, doled out Neosporin, soothed hurt feelings, worked at the Field School in Washington, D.C. to pay for children's tuitions, and...I could go on and on, but you get the idea.

And she has given me her husband, and our children, grandchildren, and great grandchildren 60+ years of devotion, love, and forgiveness.

To quote Jean Vanier: "We are not called by God to do extraordinary things, but to do ordinary things with extraordinary love." That is a good description of what Mary Ellen and all the other "witnesses" do.

Let me end by quoting from Proverbs 31:

*When one finds a worthy wife, her value is far beyond pearls.*
*Her husband, entrusting his heart to her, has an unfailing prize.*
*She brings him good, and not evil, all the days of her life.*
*She is girt about with strength, and sturdy are her arms.*
*She reaches out her hands to the poor and extends her arms to the needy.*
*She is clothed with strength and dignity, and she laughs at the days to come.*
*She opens her mouth in wisdom, and on her tongue is kindly counsel.*
*Her children rise up and praise her; her husband, too, extols her:*
*"Many are the women of proven worth, but you have excelled them all."*
*Charm is deceptive and beauty fleeting;*
*the woman who fears the LORD is to be praised.*
*Give her a reward of her labors,*
*and let her works praise her at the city gates.*

# CHAPTER II

## Childhood Beginnings

### The Journey of Life

*Anyone who imagines that bliss is normal is going to waste a lot of time running around shouting that he's been robbed. The fact is that most putts don't drop, most beef is tough, most children grow up to just be people, most successful marriages require a high degree of mutual toleration, most jobs are more often dull than otherwise.*
*Life is like an old time rail journey...delays...sidetracks, smoke, dust, cinders, and jolts, interspersed only occasionally by beautiful vistas and thrilling bursts of speed.*
*The trick is to thank the Lord for letting you have the ride.*

—GORDON B. HINCKLEY

I WAS BORN ON March 20, 1935 in The Dalles, Oregon during what my mother claimed was a late snowstorm. This was in the middle of the Great Depression and my dad, who was a carpenter by trade, had no work other than harvesting crops—strawberries, hops, potatoes, and the like during the season. For my first years we lived with Grandma and Grandpa Wilber, though I don't remember that of course.

My earliest memories are of sitting around a campfire in the evening in the fields where my parents were picking crops. I remember vaguely the wooden shacks that we lived in but not much else. My parents told me stories later that now almost seem like my own memories.

9

For example, after working digging potatoes my parents were paid partially in kind and when driving back home up over the Cascade mountains, the potatoes, which were strapped to the fender on the outside of the car, froze and were ruined. My mother was devastated because they were going to be a key part of our food supply over the winter.

I do remember stuffing newspaper inside my pants and shirt to keep warm during the winter after I started 1st grade in The Dalles. I also remember my mother boiling flour and water to make hot mush for breakfast.

I also remember going to the hospital when I was 5 years old for the removal of my appendix. For some reason my parents (probably my mother) decided to have me circumcised at the same time. Mainly what I remember is pain, firstly from the circumcision[5] and then from infection of the stitches from the appendicitis incision. I remember like yesterday being held down on a table, with no pain killer of any kind, while the infected stitches were lanced and removed. I have the scar to prove it. The doctor was a recently discharged army doctor of somewhat dubious reputation.

It wasn't all hard times. We had an oil-fired heater in the living room for heat. The bedrooms were not heated and so we slept with flannel sheets and piles of blankets. We all would gather in the living room to read, play and listen to the radio. One of my favorite memories when I was five or so was laying on the floor listening to "The Cinnamon Bear" which played before Christmas every year. My brother and I would lay on the floor and spend hours looking through the Sears catalog at all the color pictures of what seemed to be endless treasures, few of which we ever could buy.

I also remember with much joy family gatherings at Grandpa and Grandma Wilber's house both before and after we moved to Portland. In my earliest years in The Dalles I was close to my first cousins, even though they were 10 years older than I. My dad's sister, Aunt Lorena, had four children, two girls and two boys—Ena Gallatin, Retha Gallatin, JR Gallatin and Glenn Gallatin. Both Glenn and JR joined the Marine Corps at the beginning of the war and served throughout the Pacific. Glenn came home without a scratch despite being at Tarawa and a number of other island battles. JR got malaria and lots of shrapnel on Iwo Jima and other islands.

In the early years Aunt Lorena lived on a farm. I spent part of a summer with them. I don't remember much except going to the outhouse at night and waking up one morning with a cow's head sticking through the window mooing. Aunt Lorena personified kindness and a certain nuttiness. She never said a bad word about anyone and believed in the Ouija Board. I remember her séances trying to contact people dead but waiting around to speak to those who believed. Her first husband ran off and was never heard from again. She worked hard to support her family and herself. She worked in Astoria shucking oysters and spent many years in a furniture factory finishing the pieces with sanding, varnishing, etc. Her house was like a rundown antique store with her collection of dolls and whatever. It puzzled me at the time, but it became clear later that it was her faith that gave her the strength to raise her family, work hard to financially support them, and to be loving and cheerful all the while.[6]

Once in a while my dad would haul trash to the local dump and my brother and I would scrounge through the dump looking for "treasures". I found a round tin of percussion caps that I brought home and hit with a hammer on the sidewalk to hear them explode. Somewhat dumb but few thought of safety in those days.

I remember we had a party to celebrate my dad getting a job as an orderly in the TB hospital, probably about 1940. But everything changed with the start of World War II.

I started school in the Fall of 1941. I attended the local grade school in The Dalles for the 1st grade that was taught by my Grandmother Hodges. My Dad built a house just behind her house on the property and we lived with her while ours was being built.

But with the war starting at the end of 1941 my Dad got a job in Portland. My mother, brother and I stayed in The Dalles until March 1942 when my Dad was able to get us an apartment in downtown Portland. The apartment was one of several cut out of an old house. We had what was the old living room and dining room and kitchen. The bathroom was upstairs in a hallway shared by all the apartments. We lived there for six months and for part of the time Grandpa Wilber and my older cousins JR and Glenn Gallatin lived with us. We had cots stacked around the floor for sleeping. Eventually JR and Glenn joined the Marines and Grandpa Wilber moved back to The Dalles.

We moved to a rental house on SE 63rd Street in Portland where I began the 2nd grade at Mt. Tabor Grade School. I had finished the 1st grade at Shattuck Grade School in downtown Portland. We stayed on 63rd Street until after the war when the owner sold the house and we moved to SE 29th Street.

I have many memories of 63rd Street. There were a lot of kids on the block and in the summer, we played ball in the street and hide-and-seek until after dark. The Wunner family—husband, wife, and son, Harry—lived with us for a year or two to split the rent. Harry was about 5-6 years older than I was. One memory which my mother talked about all the time is when Harry held me by the ankles outside the second story window. She almost had a heart attack. We had a large side yard that we planted as a Victory Garden growing much of the vegetables that we ate. We had a coal furnace and a wood burning cook stove. One of my chores was to chop the kindling and feed the stove. My brother and I took turns shoveling coal into the furnace. I had a dog that I loved and when he died, I cried when I had to drag his lifeless body out from under the porch.

During World War II many goods were rationed. For example, each member of my family got a ration book filled with coupons. To buy something you not only needed the money but also the coupon. Things you needed coupons for included milk, sugar, meat, shoes, gas, coffee, etc. Children were allowed one pint of milk a day and adults none, for example. Other goods simply were not available. Chewing gum was one. The only one in the stores was Blackjack, which was a ghastly licorice.

I remember getting a dime a week allowance for doing my chores and going to the Montevilla area where my mother did her weekly grocery shopping and I would go to the 5 and dime store and spend the morning figuring out how best to spend my dime. Comic books, puzzles, and the like held infinite fascination for me.

When we moved in 1946, I was going into the 5th grade and I did not want to change schools. Mt. Tabor Grade School was on 60th Street, close to my old house, but a long way from the new one. I begged to stay, and my folks and the schools said ok. I took the streetcar to school and back until I got a bike in the 7th grade. During the 5th and 6th grades I had a large paper route to earn spending money and I won my first and only bike in a competition to sell new subscriptions to the paper.

During the 7th and 8th grades I worked after school and Saturdays shining shoes in Charlie Ouderkirk's barber shop across the river on the west side of Portland. When I was in the 8th grade my brother joined the army and my parents separated and then divorced. My dad moved out and I stayed with mother in the 29th Street house. The following year I started Washington High School down on SE 12th and Stark Streets.

Early that Fall I went back to Mt. Tabor School and joined a pickup football game after school was over for the day. There were several adults playing also. I tackled one of them and his knee drove one of my ribs into my right kidney puncturing it resulting in massive internal bleeding. I laid on the grassy bank while friends found my mother who came and had an ambulance take me to the hospital. I remember laying in the hospital bed, groggy, probably from drugs, listening to two doctors arguing about what to do for me. The one kept saying "he will die if you don't operate" and the other replying "he will not survive the operation." The "do-nothing" argument won out and I slowly recovered. The do-nothing doctor, Millard B. Taylor, was my great uncle by marriage and my mother swore that he saved my life.

My high school years were bittersweet. I loved sports though I was not very good at them. The accident ended my freshman year of football which I wasn't able to resume until my senior year. I played left halfback (running back) but was hampered by my poor eyesight. Without my glasses I couldn't see a pass very well and beyond a few feet things were a blur. Needless to say, after a few mistakes I sat on the bench. I was able to run track—the 440 and the relay. We placed at the state meet and that was fun. I loved baseball but I was unable to see fly balls in the sun so I couldn't play; but I did go see the Portland Beavers AAA Pacific Coast baseball team whenever I could.

I got good grades but could have done better if I had studied more. There was no one at home to push me and I got caught up in socializing with my friends. No one in my immediate family or any of the Wilber's had ever graduated from high school, let alone gone to college. In addition, my mother and her new husband, Frank Evans, worked nights so she was gone when I got home from school. She used to leave dinner for me in a steamer which made everything soggy and taste alike.

When I was 16, I bought an old 1930 Ford Model A sedan for $35 and my dad helped me take off the body and replace it with an old coupe body from the junk yard. We worked in his garage many nights. It was a fun car though cold in the winter since it only had a cloth top. I earned money for gas and entertainment by busing tables in a restaurant, working in a gas station, and delivering, by bicycle, prescriptions for a pharmacy.

During my senior year, while on the way to a night meeting of a school club, I ran over what I thought was a deep-set manhole cover at a dark intersection. I went on a few blocks and parked for the meeting. Shortly thereafter police arrived and asked whose car that was outside. I said mine and they then arrested me and took me to the local jail. It appears a car hit and knocked down a child at that intersection and then a second car ran over the child as he lay in the street. A description of the second car, given by a witness a block away, fit my car. I spent the night in jail and the next day I, my mother, my school counselor, and the juvenile officer met with the judge and I was released. They agreed that I must have hit the child but didn't realize it. He was in the hospital for some weeks but fully recovered. His family sued my insurance company, but I never found out what the result was.

My most vivid memories growing up were during the war years. Two first cousins were in the Marine Corps and an uncle was in the Air Force. I developed a real hero worship for the military. When I turned 17, I joined the 41st Infantry, Oregon National Guard, for two years. We trained one weekend a month and two weeks each summer at Fort Lewis in the state of Washington.

When I was at Fort Lewis the military begin calling up national guard units around the country for service in the Korean War. We thought sure we would be activated but it never happened. I was disappointed at the time but with hindsight I am glad.

My plan for after graduation was to go to Willamette College and study pre-law. My father had been paying $65 per month to my mother for child support and he agreed to give me that for school. But that summer Dad got sick and was first diagnosed as ulcers but later as liver cancer. He couldn't work and so there was no $65 a month for school. Worst of all, after exploratory surgery to verify the diagnosis, he died within two weeks.

During this time, I met the 16-year-old girl who would change my whole life and become my wife and companion, mother of our children, and partner in life's joys and sorrows.

We met July 15, 1953. I had just graduated from high school and she was between her junior and senior years. Her best friend was dating one of my best friends and they arranged to get us together. After several missed opportunities I went to a party she put on at her folk's place while they were away. It was crowded with her girlfriends. She served cake and after I had a piece I asked for a glass of water to "wash it down." She got the water alright but poured it over my head. I then chased her down the street and it was love at first sight. Someone asked why you asked her out after that and I said, "I was fascinated by her personality." After dating her for a while I came to love her personal morals and strength of character. Within two months we began to "go steady;" I asked her at Vista House on Crown Point. Very romantic. A year later I proposed, and we got engaged and a year after that we got married.

One of the things that impressed me most about her was

her strong faith in God. This is something I had been searching for but had not found. Despite my Grandmother Hodges being a devout Baptist, once we moved to Portland my parents never went to church again. My only times were when I played on a local Methodist church baseball team and you had to attend weekly services. I do remember going to sunrise services Easter morning at Laurelhurst Park but don't remember what prompted me.

Her faith made me begin my own search and this was aided by my going to the University of Portland for college. Since I did not have the money to go away to school, and after meeting Meme (what everybody called Mary Ellen back then) I didn't want to. She suggested I check out the local Catholic college, University of Portland. Between her example and classes at UP I quickly became convinced that Roman Catholicism was right for me. I was blessed to have some wonderful Holy Cross priests to mentor me both academically and spiritually. Michael O'Brien c.s.c. taught me freshmen English and taught me how to write clear, concise essays. But more than that he listened to my thoughts and dreams. Years later, when I was at Notre Dame, Fr. O'Brien retired there, and we saw him socially.

After receiving instructions from Fr. Sullivan at St. Cecilia's Church, in February, 1954 I was baptized in the faith. My mother and dad were not active church goers, but my mom's family were mainly hard-shelled Baptists and they hardly approved. My Grandma Wilber was a Quaker, but Grandpa Wilber and the rest of the Wilber's didn't practice any faith. I heard no complaints from any of them.

At University of Portland I came to love philosophy and decided to major in it, but I was advised that there were no jobs, so I double majored in accounting. Fr. Joseph Powers c.s.c. became an adviser and like a chaplain to our growing family.[7]

Many years later he moved to Holy Cross House at Notre Dame suffering from Lou Gehrig's Disease.

During my first two years of college I worked a number of part time jobs (bill collector for a local bank, rent-a-car clerk on the graveyard shift) to pay for tuition, books, and spending money. After my sophomore year we got married and a whole new phase of life began.

## Family Remembrances

This brief childhood memoir would be incomplete if I didn't talk about the rich family life I had with aunts, uncles, cousins, and of course, my grandparents.

My immediate family was strained by conflict between my mom and dad. They did not get along, to say the least. As we will see my dad was through and through working class with no pretensions of anything else. My mom aspired to reclaim middle class status and wanted nice clothes, hairdos, etc. She constantly nagged dad about things—remodel this or that, get treatments for his baldness, dress better, etc. Dad was proud to be a finish carpenter and from the end of the war until he died, he ran the pattern-making section of Timber Structures that made huge arch supports for airplane hangars and other similar buildings. He didn't know what to make of me. I had no talent with my hands the way he did, and this sometimes irritated him. Though we were never close, I adored him and did my best to please him.

I had two brothers, one who died before I was born and another who was 4 1/2 years older than me. My brother Darrel was born in 1932 and died 10 months later. My mother remained sad and angry about this all her life. She claimed that he died because the doctor wouldn't come out to the house unless he was paid in advance. They had no money in the depths of the Depression, so Grandma Hodges had to pawn her wedding ring. By the time they got the money it was too late. Because they had no money Darrel was buried in a pauper's grave, marked only by a brick with his name. A few years ago, we visited the cemetery in The Dalles where he was buried and couldn't find the grave. Turns out that the brick had sunk a foot beneath the ground level. We had it replaced with a new headstone.

My older brother, Millard "Buster" Wilber, was born in 1930. My mother told me the story of how her Aunt Mattie and husband tried to "buy" Buster. They couldn't have children and they were relatively well off. At this time my family was very poor, but the money offered was rejected despite the hard economic times. Buster was almost 5 years older in age which meant our relationship never got beyond the "little brat brother" teasing his "mean older brother" stage. What I remember most is our mother babying me and being harsh with him. Buster had a tough high school and quit to join the Army. He was in an airborne unit (587th parachute battalion) that dropped behind the lines during the Inchon Landing in the Korean War. He was injured with white phosphorus shells and returned home from the war as a heavy drinker which over time became alcoholism from which he died in 1977 at age 47. Shortly after returning he married Dee, a woman with two children, Bobby and Janette, and they had one more, Nanette. Unfortunately, Bus's drinking destroyed the marriage and his life. He worked at odd jobs off and on over the years and when not drinking he was a sweet guy. I have always felt bad that there was nothing I could do for him with us separated by a continent. Unfortunately, our mother enabled him by constantly bailing him out of his problems.

While I didn't see my grandparents as often after moving to Portland from The Dalles, they remain vivid in my life. I did spend part of each summer with them until my teenage years.

My mother's mother, Grandma Hodges, was born in 1884 as Mary Elizabeth Bailey, but everybody called her Lizzie. She taught first grade in The Dalles for many years and after retirement she ran a pre-school in her house. She was tall, 5'10" or so and probably 250 pounds.

Her father was a Baptist minister[8] and though he died before I was born, he was part of my life both from stories told about him and through the person of my grandmother who apparently was just like him. She was a devout Baptist, never missing church and an avid reader of the bible. At the same time, she was fun. She took me to the movies seeing cowboy and Indian films, Perils of Pauline series and the like. Once she threw her back out demonstrating to me how to do somersaults. She gave me mustard plasters on my chest for deep colds and many times made me put my head into a heated coffee can filled with Vicks and breathe deeply with a towel over my head. It did clear me out.

Grandpa and Grandma Wilber were very different. They were both quiet but gentle and treated me less like a kid and more like a young man. I helped collect eggs from the chickens, dry apricots on outdoor screens, can fruits, and even learned how to chop off a chicken's head and pluck the feathers. Grandma Wilber gave me sassafras tea to thin my blood in the spring and cod liver oil whenever she thought I looked sickly. I remember once I was listening to a radio program of cowboys and Indians and I made some remark and Grandpa (who I called Pop) said: "they (the Indians) have as much right as anybody." This stuck with me. Our town, The Dalles was almost half Native American and they were not treated well.

On my mother's side there were a number of relatives I remember, some with fondness and some not so much. My cousin, Phil Hirl, was a good friend in the early years but he lived in a small town some distance from Portland, so we didn't see much of each other in the later years. He was a nut about baseball and so was I. We liked to talk about and see the Portland Beavers. We retrieved balls from the pond at Rose City Golf Course (near our Aunt Mattie's) and sold them at the club house. He went to my graduation from Washington High School. We became reacquainted during the past 10 years, during the time we spent summers in Oregon, until he died a few years ago. We also shared a common interest in family history, and I owe much of what I know about the Bailey's to him. Our grandmothers were Bailey sisters.

The Bailey family was important in my life. They were the children of Charles and Mary Jane Stephens Bailey and the brothers and sisters of my grandmother Mary Elizabeth Bailey Jackson Hodges. Seven of them lived long lives. Charles died young and Edward, who was mentally challenged, died in his 30s.

Aunt Mattie married Millard B Taylor (Uncle Doc) in a double wedding with Aunt Cassie and her husband. They lived in Grass Valley for several years, but were in Portland all the years I remember, on 62nd and Sacramento. They had no children. She had a stroke about 1950 and was bedridden most of the time, unable to talk or recognize people, until she died, about 8-10 years later. We still visited her. Uncle Doc refused to put her in a home and instead hired full-time care while he was in his office.

Uncle Doc delivered my mother and I think also me. He too was a kind and caring person, even if somewhat brusque. He sometimes took us along on his house calls. Believe it or not doctors used to do this. We waited in the car. He played Chinese checkers with me and even let me win sometimes. He is the one who saved my life by refusing to let the other doctors to perform surgery on me. Despite being a GP, he also did surgery and I remember vividly him cutting open the fourth finger on my right hand to scrape out a deep infection. I still have the scar to prove it. Another time he saved my arm from being crooked. I broke both bones in my right wrist and the doctor in The Dalles set it in a straight cast. Four weeks later my mother took me to Portland and Uncle Doc x-rayed the wrist through the cast and saw that the bones had slipped and were growing back together crooked. He had to cut off the cast, re-break the bones and set it in a new type bent cast. Six weeks later I was fine.

There are so many memories from my childhood that there is no room in this brief memoir. Let me sum up by saying, despite early poverty, I was blessed to have so many people love me—my parents, grandparents, uncles and aunts, cousins, and high school friends that I still cherish.

## Raising a Family

On June 4, 1955 Mary Ellen and I got married in St. Cecilia's Catholic Church in Portland, Oregon. As she walked down the aisle she cried and cried. Then later after stopping, the singing of Ave Maria set her off again. While waiting in the sacristy, Fr. Michael O'Brien, c.s.c., said to me: "This is your last chance." He had been trying for the past two years to recruit me to become a priest and join the Holy Cross order. I don't think he was serious. He was famous for his dry wit. Mary Ellen thinks he was serious.

The first two years of our married life was conditioned by my finishing the last two years of school at the University of Portland. The first year Mary Ellen worked at the First National Bank. I worked at several part time jobs while going to school—bill collector for a bank, accounting clerk for an appliance manufacturer, and working for a public accounting firm. Mary Ellen got pregnant in early July and worked up to the week before delivery on April 3rd, 1956. She took the bus to work every day and during the morning sickness phase, once she had to get off the bus part way to town and heave and then get back on another bus to finish going to work.

During the final two years of college we moved three times, ending up at Columbia Villa, a public housing project in north Portland near the university. We had a two-bedroom duplex that was pretty nice. There was no insulation or storm windows, so the windows all iced up on the inside during the winter and wet diapers drying on clothes horses made the air fragrant. Mary Ellen did the wash in a wringer wash machine. She put the clothes, soap, and water in and turned it on. It agitated the load but that's all. She then put each item through the wringer one at a time by hand and then hung them up to dry. There were many married students living at the Villa, so it was a good place to be.

Our entertainment primarily consisted of playing pinochle and hearts with friends in the Villa. The couple that was at the other couple's place would dash back to their home periodically to check on their kids.

After graduation in June 1957, I got a job as a junior accountant at Haskins & Sells, the international accounting firm, in San Francisco. So, we were off to a new stage in our life, even though it was short lived.

# CHAPTER III

## Oregon and the Christian Family Movement

*How Prayer Works*
*You pray for the hungry.*
*Then you feed them. This is*
*How Prayer Works.*

—POPE FRANCIS

AFTER FINISHING my B.A. in accounting and philosophy at the University of Portland—the former to earn a living since I was married with two children when I graduated and the latter because I loved it—I worked in public accounting long enough to get my C.P.A.

After graduation in June 1957 I took a job with the international accounting firm, Haskins & Sells, in their San Francisco, California office. It was not a match made in heaven. We had two children, a son, Kenny, born April 3, 1956 and a daughter, Teresa, just born that June 8, 1957. We found a house to rent in San Mateo giving me a long commute—by train to San Francisco, then by bus to near the office, and finally a few blocks walk, adding up to about 1 1/2 hours each way. To top it off I hated my work. I had worked part time while still in school for a small accounting firm doing bookkeeping for small companies such as jewelry stores. But here I was working on large companies such as Borden Milk, doing auditing by turning checks hour after hour day after day. The financial living costs were greater than expected so we had to move from San Mateo to a second-floor walk-up apartment on Alamo Square in the Fulton District of San Francisco, which at the time was not particularly desirable. But the rent was cheap, $75, compared to San Mateo at $135.

Mary Ellen had to walk to the grocery store with two kids, return and climb the stairs with a grocery bag in one arm and the baby in the other while the 18-month-old crawled up the stairs. When she did laundry, she would have to hang the clothes to dry on a line outside a window that stretched between buildings. Serious Asian flu hit the U.S. in 1957 and I got it bad. I ran a temperature of 105 and was delirious. We didn't know anyone, so Mary Ellen called the local parish priest and he gave us the name of a doctor who prescribed lots of liquids. She had to go out at night to a liquor store and get 7up, which was a dicey thing to do since a single woman on the dark streets was a target.

Unfortunately, not only did I dislike working at Haskins & Sells, but I had to wear a suit and hat, and eat out lunch every day. Also living in San Francisco, if you are not rich, is not fun. Everything was expensive and apartment living with a family was hard. So, I contacted my old accounting professor in Portland about a job. He had a small accounting firm and he hired me to work for him. Thus, we moved back to Portland in November 1957. Mary Ellen's mother found a house in Beaverton, Oregon (a suburb of Portland) for us to rent. We moved in December 1957 driving straight through (including a snowstorm) because we did not have money for a motel. It took 20+ hours.

After settling in a new job and a new house we joined St. Cecilia's Catholic Church and became active in the Christian

Family Movement (CFM), after being recruited by the new young assistant pastor, straight from Ireland, Michael Fleming.[9] Up to this point my faith while strong was traditional: go to Sunday Mass, pray the Rosary, read edifying literature, be generous in giving to the church and to the poor. Now a concern with justice was instilled by our participation in CFM which utilized the observe-judge-act approach to bring Christian values to bear upon the problems of the social, economic, and political worlds in which we lived. Thus, as a group we tried to put those Christian teachings into practice through local action such as lobbying the state legislature for migrant labor laws and sponsoring immigration for Dutch Indonesians.

I worked in the small accounting firm doing the books and preparing tax returns for small businesses such as jewelry stores, sawmills, etc. It was much better than my earlier job at Haskins & Sells but still pretty boring. My boss was asked for a suggestion of someone to teach accounting part time at Multnomah Junior College and he thought I might enjoy doing that in addition to working for him. I jumped at the chance and taught economics and mathematics in addition to accounting. I was drawn further into economics by my desire to attain a better understanding of the causes of poverty and how to overcome it. While at the national convention of CFM at the University of Notre Dame in 1959, the national chaplain of CFM, Fr. Louie Putz, c.s.c.[10] urged me to get a master's degree. As a result, I went back to school at the University of Portland and got a M.S. degree in social science. I quit the accounting firm and taught full time while doing the master's degree.

Our continued participation in CFM taught us that we are the hands and feet of Christ in the world. We are called to serve the poor and disadvantaged, seek justice and peace, and grow in faith wherever we found ourselves—in the home, at work, through church. Through our CFM group we lobbied for laws to protect migrant workers in the strawberry fields and helped set up and sponsor a program to bring in Dutch-Indonesian refugees to the Portland area. Members of our CFM group gave talks at a number of other parishes and the idea spread to other CFM groups in the area with eventually 120 families sponsored and brought into the area. Our Beaverton CFM group sponsored a family with seven children. Through the parish we rehabbed an old house they owned, found a job for the father, and arranged for all the little details such as bus transportation to work, enrollment in schools, etc. It is important to mention that before I begin the program of speaking to other parishes about joining us in sponsoring refugees, I went to see Archbishop Howard to ask for his permission. His response was: "Don't ask, I might have to say no. Just go do it. It is your job."[11]

Most of our actions, however, were more modest and were home centered. Let me give one example. It is in families that children first learn to love their neighbors as themselves. One of the first times we taught our children this was at Christmas. After we opened our gifts, we suggested that each member of the family should select one of their gifts and give it to the local Catholic Worker house which in turn would see that the gifts went to those less fortunate than ourselves. We emphasized the obligation to share our riches with those who had none. Our oldest son, Kenny, who was four at the time, chose his most expensive present, a huge, beautiful fire engine that his grandmother had given him. We told him it wasn't necessary to give his biggest, most expensive gift. He insisted. We were rather red-faced when his grandmother asked where the fire engine was.

During this time that we were deeply involved in our local parish, particularly in its social ministry, our Christian faith became revitalized as we came to realize through study of the bible and CST that we all are called to do God's work in this world. To love God is to love neighbor:

> Those who say, 'I love God', and hate their brothers or sisters, are liars; for those who do not love a brother or sister- whom they have seen, cannot love God whom they have not seen. The commandment we have from him is this: those who love God must love their brothers and sisters also. (1Jn: 4, 19-20)

## The Biblical Tradition

The strong emphasis in the Old Testament prophets calling for social justice and condemning excessive and irresponsible wealth changed my way of seeing the world. Central to the biblical view is that justice in a community is most directly tested by its treatment of the powerless in society, most often described as the widow, the orphan, the poor and the stranger (non-Israelite) in the land. The prophets continually call the king and the people back to commitment to justice for the powerless. They direct scathing attacks at the rich and powerful who "sell the just man for silver, and the poor man for a pair of sandals. They trample the heads of the weak into the dust of the earth and force the lowly out of the way" (Am. 2:6-7). Isaiah pronounces God's judgment on those "who have devoured the vineyard; the loot wrested from the poor is in your houses" (3:14). Jeremiah condemns the man "who builds his house on wrong, his terraces on injustice." He praises King Josiah because "he dispensed justice to the weak and the poor." Jeremiah then adds the startling statement: "Is this not true knowledge of me? says the Lord" (22:16). He then adds, "your eyes and heart are set on nothing except on your own gain" (22:17). Thus, doing of justice is equated with knowledge of the Lord. The practice of justice is constitutive of true belief. And the pursuit of self-interest is seen as a stumbling block to knowing and serving God. At the beginning of Lent, a reading from Isaiah 58: 5-7 proclaims:

> Is this the manner of fasting I wish,
> of keeping a day of penance:
> That a man bow his head like a reed,
> and lie in sackcloth and ashes?
>
> ...
>
> This, rather, is the fasting I wish:
> releasing those bound unjustly,
> untying the thongs of the yoke;
> Setting free the oppressed,
> breaking every yoke;
> Sharing your bread with the hungry,
> sheltering the oppressed and the
> homeless;
> Clothing the naked when you see them,
> and not turning your back on your
> own.

If Jesus is, as Christians claim, Lord and the son of God, then he is Lord of every aspect of our lives, including the economic one, and his teaching and example must have some relevance to economics as well. In fact, Jesus followed in the prophetic tradition, taking the side of those who are powerless or on the margin of his society such as the tax collectors (Lk. 15:12), the widow (Lk. 7:11-17; Mk. 12:41-44), the Samaritan (Lk. 17:11-19), the sinful woman (Lk 7:36-50), and children (Mk. 10:13-16). Jesus' description of the final judgment in Matthew 25 (31-46) still haunts me with its powerful message of what it means to be a Christian:

> "Lord, when did we see you hungry and feed you, or thirsty and give you drink? When did we see you a stranger and welcome you, or naked and clothe you? When did we see you ill or in prison, and visit you?" And the king will say to them in reply, "Amen, I say to you, whatever you did for one of these least brothers of mine, you did for me."

The concern with justice was reinforced by CFM's observe-judge-act methodology to bring Christian values to bear upon the problems of the social, economic, and political worlds in which we live. The observe-judge-act approach was first developed by Cardinal Joseph Cardijn, when he was a parish priest in Belgium before World War II. He inspired many Catholic social action groups such as the Young Christian Workers, Young Christian Students, and the Christian Family Movement.

In CFM, five or six married couples would meet every two weeks for two hours. The meeting would consist of two basic parts, a scriptural inquiry and a social inquiry. The scriptural inquiry consists of reflecting on a specific bible passage related to the social inquiry topic. The social inquiry part of each session utilizes the observe-judge-act approach. It works in the following way. We *observe* a situation from daily life, *judge* whether or not the situation needs to be changed and agree to *act*. Observations are most often information obtained by consulting various sources. These facts are events, such as the county raised property taxes, statistics, such as the percentage unemployed in our county increased to 10 percent; opinions of others, such as five out of seven neighbors you talked with think more funds need to be spent on the local high school; or your own experiences, such as "where I work men get promoted ahead of women even when the women are clearly more qualified." The sources of facts are important, of course. Sources from several different places, such as both Fox News and CNN, will usually give a better view of reality.

While the observe section tries to answer the question, "What is really going on here?" the judge section uses our Christian faith to evaluate the reality observed and answer the question, "How can we make it better?" We make it better when we are able to advance human dignity. The culmination of each meeting is the selection of an appropriate action.

The best actions are those that grow out of the group's discussion of the observations and the judgments from using CST to evaluate those observations. The actions suggested are just that—suggestions. The members need to feel comfortable with the actions they choose. They don't have to be major; they have to be heartfelt. They might range from writing a letter to your senator to getting your parish to start a food pantry and everything in between.

This is an example taken from my small book entitled *Catholics Spending and Acting Justly*:[12]

****************

## SCRIPTURAL REFLECTION

*Proverbs* 14: 21, 31

*Matthew* 25: 31-46

*Reflect on what the hungry, the stranger, the naked, the sick, and the prisoner share in common? Why do you think Jesus identifies with the poor— " whatever you did for one of these least brothers of mine, you did for me.?" Reflect on the times you have served Christ without knowing it. Does this impact your view of what it means to be a Christian?*

## SOCIAL INQUIRY

Poverty is not an isolated problem existing solely among a small number of anonymous people in our central cities. Nor is it limited to a dependent underclass or to specific groups in the United States. It is a condition experienced at some time by many people of different walks of life and in different circumstances. Many poor people are working but at wages insufficient to lift them out of poverty. Others are unable to work and are therefore dependent on outside sources of support. Still others are on the edge of poverty: although not officially defined as poor, they are economically insecure and at the risk of falling into poverty.

As the U.S. Bishops said: "The themes of human dignity and the preferential option for the poor are at the heart of our approach; they compel us to confront the issue of poverty with a real sense of urgency." (*Economic Justice for All*, §186) Overcoming poverty is not a luxury to which we can deal with when we find the time and resources. Rather, it is a moral priority of the highest order.

Poor and homeless people sleep in community shelters and in our church basements. The hungry fill soup kitchens. Unemployment gnaws at the self-respect of both middle-aged persons who have lost their jobs and the young who cannot find them. Hardworking men and women wonder if the system of enterprise that helped them yesterday might destroy their jobs and their communities tomorrow. Ethnic minorities often face racism, which may inhibit their full participation in the economic sphere. Now retired, many elderly are alone, and their families struggle financially to care for them.

Although the precise determination of who lives in poverty may be questioned, some trends can still be traced. Poverty exists both transitionally and transgenerationally. Each type has its distinct causes, and each affects individuals differently. Although there is some overlap, the solutions for the elimination of each type is particular to the type of the poverty.

Transitional poverty, usually of a more temporary duration, results when an individual living above the poverty line falls below. Divorce, widowhood, retirement, unemployment, or illness may financially bind a previously economically stable person. While some struggle to overcome adversity without success, others in transitional poverty move out of their financial distress, either by their own efforts or with the help of others.

Transgenerational poverty, on the other hand, develops among children who, because they grow up in poverty, do not have equal access to adequate health care, proper nutrition, or quality education. When pregnant women and young children lack necessary care, the youngsters will often suffer from lower intellectual abilities and missed days at school. Those who may receive satisfactory health benefits may still struggle in under-funded schools, which cannot provide the necessary supplies or attention the youths require. Without an education, these children often follow their parents work history: they find employment at low paying jobs, if they qualify for any position at all. These inequalities, thus, contribute to continuing the cycle of poverty.

Those living in transgenerational poverty are not only materially poor; they also often lack the necessary education, job opportunities, and psychological tools to lift themselves out of their situation. Economic poverty can cause alienation from mainstream society, leading to destitution of other sorts, often more serious than the initial financial inadequacies. The lack of hope for change and loss of meaning in life, which is so evident in the lives of many poor, are the true tragedies of economic poverty.

Economic arrangements can be the source of fulfillment, of hope, and of community, or they may be the roots of frustration, isolation, and even despair. The economic sphere affects the quality of people's lives, even whether people live or die. Serious economic choices go beyond purely technical issues to fundamental questions of value and purpose. People learn the virtues and vices; they derive meaning for their lives; they define themselves by the roles played in the economic world. As Christians, we believe that, in facing these questions, the Christian religious and moral tradition as embodied in Catholic Social Thought is instrumental in determining which direction we should head.

Sustaining a common culture and commitment to moral values is essential if the economy is to serve all people more fairly. Many Americans feel themselves in the grip of economic demands and cultural pressures that go far beyond the individual's, or even the family's, capacity to cope. Decision-making within corporations too often focuses only on the profit of the company, often to the detriment of workers or the environment. Government policies, which affect the quality of life of nearly every American, must be determined with the common good in mind.

However, this vision of the common good is not easily achieved. In combating poverty, we are tempted to find the solutions only in terms of economics and policy change. Too often, we see poverty as a pervasive problem about which we can do nothing personally. Faced with this, the Church proclaims that individuals, as sacred and social beings, must do what is within their power to eliminate poverty. Neglecting this personal responsibility is contrary to the Body of Christ and the Gospels.

**Observe**

1. Go to http://www.nccbuscc.org/cchd/povertyusa/index.htm where you will information on poverty in the United States. See if you find information that you didn't know and surprises you. Share your findings with the group.
2. Try to find out who are the poor in your parish, in your neighborhood, your town. What is being done to help them by private groups and through public programs.
3. Find out what programs for the poor are sponsored by your parish and what ones could be.
4. Is there a need for clothing in your community? What do you do with clothing you no longer wear?
5. If you became homeless what would you most miss about your home?
6. If you know a family where there is a serious illness describe the effect on the family members.

7. This is a true story.[13] A young man in New York was
   coming home from work on a cold night when he passed
   a beggar who asked for a dollar to buy food. He ignored
   the beggar because he assumed the money would be
   wasted on alcohol instead of food. But after getting home
   his conscience began to bother him and he made a bowl
   of soup. He brought it to the beggar and sat it down
   without saying a word. From then on he did this every
   night which soon attracted several more beggars. So he
   cooked even more soup. One night he brought a whole
   gallon of hot split-pea soup, set it down and turned to go.
   One of the beggars grabbed the jar of soup and broke it
   over the young man's head. He was shocked and asked:
   "Why did you do that?" The beggar replied: "You are
   doing nothing more than bringing food to the dogs.
   Why don't you talk with us; we don't bite." Reflect on
   this story and come prepared to discuss it at the meeting.
   Have you experienced an incident where a kind person
   helped you but didn't respect you?

**Judge**

1. In reference to observe number seven how was the beggar's
   behavior wrong? Did the young man misunderstand
   the meaning of charity? Can you think of lessons that
   the beggar taught the young man about the Church's social
   teaching?
2. If your income decreased sharply how would you
   prioritize what to do without?
3. What changes would you make to society's help for the
   poor?
4. Does everyone have a right to affordable housing and
   medical care?

**Act** (here are some suggestions but feel free to come up with your own)

1. Go to http://www.nccbuscc.org/cchd/povertyusa/involved.
   shtml and read about all the ways you can get involved in

your community. Choose one and report back to the group on your success.
2. Using the information from one above return to the group with a suggestion for a group action.
3. Visit a local shelter and volunteer to help prepare and serve a meal or some other needed service.
4. Make a list of all the volunteer possibilities in your community and make this available to the whole parish.

******************

The above is just one example of how Catholic action can be generated. In addition, by incorporating some of the aspects of the Comunidades de Base,[14] family based Catholic action groups can be strengthened. These communities are the basic unity of the Church where deeper prayer and shared values are lived, where personal and group objectives merge to question, discuss and act, and where ordinary people are given a sense of being the Church as a leaven in society and the world. Members of these small groups of Christians have a sense of responsibility for themselves as they celebrate the faith together. They form the Church as God's People rather than God's building.

Thus, while still innocent of graduate level economic theory, I begin to study the specifically Christian approach to the economy embodied in CST and tried to put those teachings into practice through local action such as the already mentioned work of lobbying the state legislature for migrant labor laws, sponsoring immigration for Dutch-Indonesians, and working in soup kitchens.

### The Catholic Social Thought Tradition

Let me sketch-in the tradition of CST that I learned. In the late 1950s and early 1960s, it was the encyclicals of Leo XIII and Pius XI that were the standard readings. Then over the next 30+ years John XXIII, Paul VI, and John Paul II added many new encyclicals that reinforced the fundamentals and expanded their scope. For example, it was John XXIII who first applied CST to the developing world. At the present time, Pope Francis's encyclicals have focused on poverty and inequality within the context of environmental issues. My summary here includes what I learned at that time and what came later.

As I briefly mentioned in Chapter 1, CST is rooted in a commitment to certain fundamental values—the right to human dignity, the need for human freedom and partici-pation, the importance of community, and the nature of the common good. These values are drawn from the belief that each person is called to be a co-creator with God, participat-ing in the redemption of the world and the furthering of the Kingdom. This requires social and human development where the religious and temporal aspects of life are not separated and opposed to each other.

As a result of these fundamental values two principles permeate CST. The first is a special concern for the poor and powerless which leads to a criticism of political and economic structures that oppress them. The second is a concern for cer-tain human rights against the collectivist tendencies of the state and the neglect of the free market.

Ever since *Rerum Novarum* [RN][15] in 1891, CST has taught that both state socialism and free market capitalism vio-late these principles. State socialism denies the right of private property, excites the envy of the poor against the rich leading to class struggle instead of cooperation, and violates the proper order of society by the state usurping the role of individuals and social groups [RN, 7-8; *Centesimus Annus* [CA], 13-14] .[16] Free market capitalism denies the concept of the common good and the "social and public character of the right of property" [*Quadragesimo Anno* [QA], 46], including the principle of the universal destination of the earth's goods [RN, 14; CA, 6]; and violates human dignity by treating labor merely as a commodity to be bought and sold in the marketplace [RN, 31; QA, 83; CA, 33-35]. Pope John Paul II summarizes the thrust of CST when he says: "The individual today is often suffocated between two poles represented by the State and the marketplace. At times it seems as though he exists only as a producer and consumer of goods, or as an object of State administration. People lose sight of the fact that life in society has neither the market nor the State as its final purpose, since life itself has a unique value which the State and the market must serve" [CA, 49].

The concept of the common good in CST emphasizes both the dignity of the human person and the essentially social nature of that dignity. Both civil and political liberties on the one hand and social and economic needs on the other are essential components of the common good. The common good is not the aggregate of the welfare of all individuals. Rather it is a set of social conditions necessary for the realization of human dignity which transcend the arena of private exchange and contract. Such conditions or goods are essentially relational. To exist they must exist as shared. In short, individual persons have rights to those things necessary to realize their dignity as human beings. CST argues further that in pursuing the common good, special concern must be given to the economy's impact on the poor and powerless because they are particularly vulnerable and needy [CA, 11].

Pope John XXIII, in his encyclical *Pacem in Terris* [PT], set out in detail a full range of human rights that can only be realized and protected in solidarity with others. These rights include the civil and political rights to freedom of speech, worship, and assembly. He also includes a number of economic rights concerning human welfare. First among these are the rights to life, food, clothing, shelter, rest, medical care, and basic education. In order to ensure these rights everyone has the right to earn a living. Everyone also has a right to security in the event of illness, unemployment, or old age. The right to participate in the community requires the right of employment, as well as the right to healthful working conditions, wages, and other benefits sufficient to support families at a level in keeping with human dignity [PT, 8-27; CA, 8, 15].

CST repudiates the position that the level of unemployment, the degree of poverty, the quantity of environmental destruction, and other such outcomes should be left to the dictates of the market. Emphasis on the common good means that the community has an obligation to ensure the right of employment to all persons [CA, 15], to help the disadvantaged overcome their poverty [CA, 19, 40], and to safeguard the environment. [CA, 37].

Although CST defends the right to private ownership of productive property [RN, 10, 15, 36], the common good sometimes demands that this right be limited by the community through state regulation, taxation, and even, under exceptional circumstances, public ownership [Popularum Progressio [PP], 23]. The attainment and safeguarding of human rights sometimes require the overriding of market outcomes. Therefore, CST insists that "government has a moral function: protecting human rights and securing basic justice for all members of the commonwealth" [PT, 60-62]. Pope John Paul II says society and the state have the duty of "defending the basic rights of workers," defending those "collective and qualitative needs which cannot be satisfied by market mechanisms," and "overseeing and directing the exercise of human rights in the economic sector" [CA, 40, 48].

Catholic thought sees society as made up of a dense network of relations among individuals, families, churches, neighborhood associations, business firms, labor unions, and different levels of government. Thus, every level of society has a role to play in ensuring basic human rights and the common good. In CST this is expressed as the "principle of subsidiarity:"

> Just as it is gravely wrong to take from individuals what they can accomplish by their own initiative and industry and give it to the community, so also it is an injustice and at the same time a grave evil and disturbance of right order to assign to a greater and higher association what lesser and subordinate organizations can do. For every social activity ought of its very nature to furnish help (subsidium) to the members of the body social, and never destroy and absorb them [QA, 79; also, CA, 15].

This principle provides for a pluralism of social actors. Each, from the individual person to the federal government, has obligations. Higher levels should not usurp the authority of lower levels except when necessary. However, the principle works both ways. When individuals, families, or local communities are unable to solve problems that undermine the common good, the state governments are obligated to intervene, and if their resources and abilities are inadequate, then the federal government assumes the responsibility. This principle also extends into the international economy. As Pope John Paul II says, "this increasing internationalization of the economy ought to be accompanied by effective international agencies which will oversee and direct the economy to the common good, something that an individual State, even if it were the most powerful on earth, would not be in a position to do" [CA, 58].

The right to private property and the principle of subsidiarity limit the role of the state while the principle of solidarity [CA, 15] requires that society and the state intervene in markets to protect human rights, particularly of the poorest. The thrust of CST, therefore, has been to repudiate both state socialism and free market capitalism.

Since the primary "signs of the times" that Pope John Paul II focused on in CA, published in 1991, was the collapse of Communism in Eastern Europe, he emphasized the limits to the role of the state and the utility of markets in providing incentives for production. However, this was a highly qualified endorsement as when he says the efficiency of markets in fulfilling human needs is true only for those needs which are "'solvent', insofar as they are endowed with purchasing power, and for those resources which are 'marketable', insofar as they are capable of obtaining a satisfactory price. But there are many human needs which find no place on the market." [CA, 34] Thus, markets do not adequately fulfill the needs of those who have little income or provide for non-marketable goods such as a clean environment and participation in the workplace. He also registered his fears about the impact of markets on the "human environment" [CA, 38-39] and their role in creating "consumerism." [CA, 36]

What actual economic system does CST endorse? Explicitly, none. As Pope John Paul II says: "The Church has no models to present" [CA, 43] of the best economic system; that is for history to decide in each individual case. However, he did carefully distinguish between free market capitalism, which he criticizes, and a socially regulated version he calls "the new capitalism". Free market capitalism fails to provide adequate housing, medical care, education, socio-economic security, and meaningful participation in economic life for all families, including the poorest. [CA, 33] Its unrestrained profit motive results in environmental destruction [CA, 37], promotes a soulless consumerism [CA, 36], and destroys the human environment needed by a community of persons. [CA, 38] It is social regulation, guided by the principles of subsidiarity and solidarity, that can overcome the injustices of free market capitalism. The degree of regulation is not a matter of principle but rather a case of prudential judgment in particular cases.

Some argue that the U.S. economy comes closest to resembling the ideal of the new capitalism envisaged in *Centesimus Annus.* It is true that the economic policies and social welfare measures enacted from the 1930s through the 1960s tamed the worst consequences of free market capitalism. Macroeconomic stabilization policies reduced average unemployment levels, social security enhanced the life of the elderly, and various income maintenance programs helped the very poor. However, this regulated market economy came under attack during the 1980s from a free market philosophy that was resurrected with the election of Ronald Reagan as president.[17] Government programs established during the previous 45 years were attacked because they supposedly reduced incentives and thus productivity. Free up the economy and all would be well. Reduce welfare, minimum wages, and unemployment benefits so that the poor would have greater incentives to work. Lower taxes and remove regulations on business so that the resulting higher profits would encourage corporations and wealthy individuals to save and invest. Increased productivity and growth in GDP would result. Eventually, the benefits would trickle down so that even those on the bottom would be better off than before. This vision of the world—where free individuals pursue their self-interest to the greater good of all—is at odds both with the results of economic policies since the 1980s and with much of CST.

The more that I studied CST and the more we participated in CFM, the more I became convinced that a career in accounting is not what I wanted. Fr. Michael Fleming,[18] who organized our CFM group and became our chaplain, and one of the members, Ed Smith,[19] became powerful influences in my life through their knowledge of Catholic thought and intense personalities. Our wide ranging and intense discussions fed my desire to know more and to do more.

In the summer of 1959, Mary Ellen and I took the train to South Bend, Indiana for the CFM national conference held at the University of Notre Dame. There we met all kinds of people who were dedicating their lives to be the hands and feet of Christ in the world in which they found themselves. Of particular note were Pat and Patty Crowley,[20] Dan and Rose Lucey,[21] Estelle and Mario Carota,[22] and Fr. Louie Putz, C.S.C.[23]

The Crowley's were the national chair couple of CFM and the dynamic leaders for many years. After the conference they drove us back to their home in Chicago where we spent the night and caught the train the next morning to go back home to Oregon. It was a fascinating night. There had to be at least 25-30 people spending the night, most sleeping on the floor in a variety of rooms. The Carota's with their 17 children, eleven adopted, slept in the basement and early the next morning left in their homemade camper bus. They had just returned from Mexico where they led a building project in the slums of Tacuba. They ran an apple farm in Aptos, California that they named Agnus Dei Farm, where they raised their children and entertained many guests.

The Lucey's were an incredibly energetic couple who always seemed to turn their sorrows and setbacks into joy and, in turn, the joy into action for peace and justice. They "visited five continents and wrote The Living Loving Generation. Dan and Rose started the San Ysidro Shop bookstores in Canoga

Park, Torrance, and Oakland, CA, even though Dan worked full time for the Post Office and Rose had nine children to care for."[24]

Fr. Louie Putz, C.S.C., who became a close friend years later when we moved to South Bend, played a key role in my life. When I talked with him, during the conference, about my vague ideas of working in the missions or some such thing, as noted earlier, he said go back to school and get your master's degree. I did just that, which enabled me to move from part time to full time teaching at Multnomah College in Portland. And that experience helped me to get the offer to teach in Ponce, Puerto Rico. The rest, as they say, is history.

# CHAPTER IV

# Lay Missionaries in Puerto Rico

*Do not be daunted by the enormity*
*of the world's grief.*
*Do justly, now. Love mercy, now.*
*Walk humbly, now.*
*You are not obligated to complete the work,*
*but neither are you free*
*to abandon it.*

—The Talmud

DURING 1959-60, I was becoming dissatisfied with my work, feeling I needed to do more. Both my faith, reinforced by our CFM experiences, and my sense of adventure led me to look for ways of satisfying both. I wrote to many places about working in the missions in Latin America but in those days, there was little to no financial support for lay people. Finally, a letter sent to the Mission Secretariat of the United States Catholic Welfare Conference (as it was then known) was answered with an offer of a job teaching at the Catholic University of Puerto Rico in Ponce. My letter crossed their desk just when Msgr. Ivan Illich,[25] the vice-rector of the university was passing through. He made me an offer. I was to teach accounting, economics, and mathematics. I accepted with enthusiasm, Mary Ellen somewhat less so seeing as she was pregnant with our fourth child. Alice was born August 8, 1960 and baptized by Fr. Fleming at St. Cecilia's. Her Godparents were

Bob and Ursula Cogan, good CFM friends. Due to a mix-up, I assumed that school started in Puerto Rico after Labor Day, same as in Oregon. However, we found out at the last moment that school there started mid-August. Thus, I had

LEAVING PORTLAND archdiocese for lay missionary work in far-away lands are these families from left, Mr. and Mrs. Charles Wilber of St. Cecilia parish, Beaverton, and Matt, 16 months old; Kenny, 4; and Terry, 3. Mr. and Mrs. Reid Cerny of Salem and Benedict, 18 months old; and Mr. and Mrs. Henry Woods of Roseburg. Their ultimate destinations are Puerto Rico, possibly South America and

to leave by myself two days after Alice was born. We had sold our house and most furnishings and were living in the guest house of Carolyn and Phil Dellwo, CFM friends of ours. I flew to Puerto Rico by myself (a very bumpy ride that left almost everyone air sick) and Mary Ellen was to come 2 1/2 weeks later, *by herself with four children including a three-week-old baby.* I quickly sent a letter to her saying she needed help when she came.

The story of Mary Ellen's trip to Puerto Rico is best told in her own words: "Before leaving I received a letter...saying I had to bring someone with me such as my mother. He didn't say why but my mother made some remark like, probably those Puerto Rican men! I assumed it was because of a bumpy airplane flight from New York to Puerto Rico. I decided to go it alone—that is with four children ranging in age from 4 years to 3 weeks. It turned out to be a nightmare. We changed planes in New York, and we were met there by a friend of someone at the university. He was just out of jail for anti-war activities. Nice guy though. He got us on the plane, but we left behind a baby carrier. The plane ride to Puerto Rico from New York was fine except the stewardess was cranky and never offered to help. Finally, a kindly lady took two of the kids and read to them. We arrived at the San Juan airport and we were met by Chuck and a Marianist Brother from the university telling us it was a 4 1/2-hour drive to Ponce through winding mountain roads. By the time we got there it had been more than 24 hours of sleepless travel. During the drive to Ponce, Kenny got car sick and heaved the whole way. This was our first use of disposable diapers. He heaved and we tossed. Just before arriving at our house Chuck said don't be afraid but there are a few problems. There are lizards all over the walls but don't worry they eat mosquitoes. Also, the tub and toilet are stained but don't worry they are clean."

During the three weeks that I was in Ponce before the rest of the family arrived there was a lot to do. The university was staffed primarily with priests and nuns of various religious orders and local lay people. The university had built houses on campus for each of the orders. I lived with the Marianist priests until I found a house for the family. There were few options for family housing. The vast majority of places consisted of one room on stilts that you could buy for less than $100, however, no running water or plumbing. The other choice was a small concrete block house that was very expense relative to our income. I finally rented a 600 square foot house with three bedrooms, bath, living area/dining room, and tiny kitchen. There was also a walled yard with a wash house out back with a room for a maid. The rent was $135 a month and my salary was $300 a month so things were not flush. There was no furniture or appliances in the house but the father of the other family from the States, who worked as the maintenance director, scrounged up everything we needed—beds, table and chairs, kitchen stove and refrigerator, even a washing machine. The stove had no knobs, so he made them out of wood.

During that first week in Puerto Rico some nuns came to the house bringing candles, saying a hurricane was headed directly toward Ponce. This was a first for us. They told us to be prepared by getting ready to close the shutters and stay inside in a safe place. Fortunately for us the hurricane only hit us at a glance, and we had no damage.

It was an exciting year we spent in Puerto Rico. Mary Ellen had her hands full with four children, four years and under. Cooking was a major chore with a makeshift stove, weevils in the flour, unfamiliar produce, and sky-high prices on foods shipped from the states. Washing also had its difficulties. The washing machine was outside in a shed like structure and clothes had to be hung up to dry. The afternoon rains meant you hung up clothes earlier in the day. A greater problem was during the month-long harvest season for sugar cane when the fields were burned to make it easier to harvest. Black soot hung in the air day after day. The first time it happened we were caught unawares, and the clothes became black and had to be rewashed and hung up to dry in the house. This created another small problem in that the window slats had to be kept closed so the soot wouldn't pour in but it still drifted in. The heat and humidity became almost unbearable and it took the clothes forever to dry.

The children adjusted better than we did to the new environment. Kenny quickly became fluent in Spanish for a four-year-old and acted as our translator with the street kids and some of our neighbors. Orphan children ran in packs begging at houses for food. We let them come into the yard and eat from the many fruit trees. Teresa sold one of them Mary Ellen's watch for a penny. With neighbor girls she went around the block and somehow returned with no shoes. We never did find them. We kidded Matt that a neighbor girl, Molly-olly, was his girlfriend. One day Kenny took off unbeknown to us and followed a parade downtown. I and a neighbor searched and found him and brought him home. His response was: "Why are you upset; I wasn't lost."

I taught accounting and mathematics at the university and did the daily English language news broadcast on the university radio station. The classes were taught in English, but the students were all raised speaking Spanish. Their English was not very good, but my Spanish was worse. This made for difficult times making me feel at times like a classic gringo colonizer. One of my older students, who was a member of the Independence Party, often challenged my "do-gooder" mentality; that, in fact, I represented the colonial power of the United States. I found it difficult to refute his arguments.

We both worked with a local order of nuns helping to distribute used clothes that our Beaverton CFM people mailed down to us. We also used funds sent by the monks of Our Lady of Guadalupe Trappist Abbey in Lafayette, Oregon to help the local nuns in their work.

Unfortunately, the local parish was not interested in social justice issues. The church was new, an architectural wonder that was displayed on the front page of Life magazine. When we registered, we noticed that behind the priest's desk on a wall chart was a price list for church services, such as baptisms, weddings on different days and times, etc. When we raised the issue of such a fancy church building and charging the poor for services, the reply was "the church may have been born in a stable, but it didn't stay there." He also explained that the statue of the "Black Madonna" was kept out of sight because some of their more important parishioners were offended by it.

We started a CFM group with four other families, two from Puerto Rico, one from Mexico, and one from the States. It provided us with spiritual and emotional support but did not lead to any significant actions.

I also worked with Msgr. Ivan Illich at his Center for Intercultural Communications. This was set up in 1956 to introduce priests and nuns, going to serve in Latin America, to the language and culture they would encounter. He was a fascinating guy. He used to come over about 11pm and stay until 2-3am talking endlessly about things in Puerto Rico and how to overcome poverty. He was the vice-chancellor of the university but refused to lead the standard lifestyle of the other priests and nuns on campus. At one point he lived with one particular order of priests in their house on campus but slept on the floor and ate only beans and rice instead of their full course meals. They got so upset with him that they forced him to leave. He then bought a one room "house" on stilts for $35, with no running water or electricity. He slept and said Mass there for the poor people in the neighborhood.[26] He left Puerto Rico after the elections in November 1960 as the local bishops opposed the Popular Democratic Party and endorsed a Christian Democratic Party that Illich spoke out against. He went on to start the new intercultural institute in Cuernavaca, Mexico. He invited me to join him there when I finished a PhD in economics. He insisted that if I wanted to be heard I had to go back to school for the PhD. That is what made us leave after only one year. Being a "hick" from Oregon I assumed you could do a PhD in one year, so I asked for a leave with every intention of returning there or to Cuernavaca. More on that later.

With Msgr Illich's urging I applied to four schools to study for a PhD in economics. I had two problems in searching for a school. We had only a little money to travel to a school, so it had to be on the east coast and I knew nothing about economics graduate programs. My undergraduate degree was in philosophy and accounting and my master's degree was in social science with some economics. So, I went to the school library and looked at catalogs, of which there were not very many. I ended up applying to four schools. I received assistantships at the University of Maryland and Syracuse University, acceptance but no aid from Harvard, and was rejected by Johns Hopkins. Maryland was much closer (and they paid more) than Syracuse in upstate New York so I accepted their offer with the intention of concentrating on the problems of development in Third World countries. Since the assistantship required me to teach two courses and I knew little economics, I read and studied Paul Samuelson's introductory textbook for the remaining time on the island.

# CHAPTER V

# Maryland and the Civil Rights Movement, 1961-68

*We shall hew out of the mountain of despair, a stone of hope.*
—MARTIN LUTHER KING, JR

WE GOT A RIDE FROM the University to San Juan where we took a plane to Washington, D.C. We mailed in boxes all we couldn't carry on the plane, arriving in mid-August. We were fortunate that friends, Hans and Madeline Furth,[27] from Oregon had recently moved to Washington, D.C. and had a large house, allowing us to stay with them for three weeks. I remember three things during our stay with the Furth's.

First and least important, Mary Ellen and I shared a twin bed so small that to turn over you had to ask the other to turn over at the same time.

Second, and a highlight for me was while we were there, Dorothy Day[28] of Catholic Worker fame, stayed for the weekend while attending a conference or some such thing. We spent a lot of time sitting around talking about social issues such as poverty in the U.S. and in the poor countries of the world. As a young know-it-all I argued that what Latin America needed was revolution. Kindly but firmly she countered with Christian love[29] and non-violence. It took me some years to truly appreciate her argument. Much of the time she sat holding our daughter Alice, who was just one year old, on her lap. I can't help but believe that this contributed to Alice becoming a social activist.

Finally, I remember the frustration of apartment hunting. My assistantship covered tuition and paid $1800 (for nine months) for teaching two courses while taking three courses. In my naiveté I assumed $75 a month for food, another $75 for rent, and $50 to cover everything else. Well, that was dumb. Everything in Washington was more expensive than I had thought it would be. Hans and I went apartment hunting and people just laughed when they saw how much I was making. Finally, Hans convinced me to exaggerate and put down $6000 a year income. But with four kids they still wouldn't rent to us.

However, we were particularly fortunate that Msgr Illich arranged a job for me at the United States Catholic Education Association for the final six weeks of summer 1961. This enabled us to earn some badly needed funds and search for a place to live.

It was clear we had to get more income, so I went through the yellow pages of the phone book under schools and began calling colleges and universities to see if they needed part-time teachers. By the time I reached the T's with nary a hope, panic was starting to set in. But when I called Trinity College,[30] an elite Catholic women's college, they were immediately interested. I went for an interview and was offered the job but with a catch—it was full time or nothing. They had lost a teacher just that week and school started the next week. It required teaching four courses each semester and paid $6000 per year. This was a life saver, so I had to say yes. There was a complication—I was already committed to teach two courses at Maryland in addition to going to graduate school full time. Oh well, the bravery (and foolhardiness) of youth said full speed ahead. Teaching six courses and taking three did take a toll on my health and meant Mary Ellen got little help from me around the house or with the kids.

With a guaranteed income we managed to rent half of an old house made into a duplex located in Tacoma Park, outside of D.C. near the University area. We lived there for about a year during which Mary Ellen became pregnant with our fifth child, Mary. We had moved from the first floor flat to the second floor because it had more bedroom space but now, we needed even more space.

We were fortunate to find a house in Riverdale, Maryland, that was large enough for our growing family and cheap enough that we could afford it. There was a problem, however. We needed a down payment which we didn't have. But our friends, Hans and Madeline Furth, lent us the money. Then we applied for an FHA loan which was first denied. I went to the loan officer and he agreed to change the evaluation on the grounds that as a teacher I had a steady income. Those were the days—little bureaucracy! The house started off as just a few rooms and over the years, rooms were added so it was somewhat "jerry" built when we bought it. It had a large yard with a small house that we rented out. It fit us well.

That first year back in the states was difficult to say the least. Moving from Puerto Rico we came with suitcases and some mailed boxes of things. One thing we did not have was warm winter clothes. Mary Ellen did miracles making clothes and buying used clothes from Goodwill, Salvation Army, and St. Vincent de Paul.

Graduate school turned out to be challenging, to say the least. During the Fall 1961 semester, I took three graduate courses at Maryland, taught two sections of introductory economics there, and taught four courses at Trinity College in Washington. The Spring 1962 semester was easier since I dropped my assistantship at Maryland. Thus, I only took three courses at Maryland and taught four at Trinity. I will expand on the academic side of my life in the next chapter.

Looking back, I'm not sure how I did it, but youth is adaptable. Also, during those three years I belonged to the local Congress of Racial Equality (CORE) group. We frequently spent our lunch hours "sitting in" the segregated restaurants along US 1 that ran by the university. We successfully integrated most of them with little opposition and no violence. We were less successful in integrating the new Bel Aire housing subdivision. There our group got put in jail though I left just before the police raided our picket line since I had promised Mary Ellen, I wouldn't get arrested and leave her with all the children. My one regret is I didn't seize the opportunity to go on a bus of "freedom riders" to Selma in the summer. The most inspiring event at this time was the 1963 March on Washington, which I participated in with other CORE members.

Clearly, the period, 1962 to August 1968, that we lived in Riverdale was a momentous time in our lives and in the life of the country. Mary, Angie, and Louie rounded out our family and the civil rights movement transformed the country.

Mary was born July 24, 1962, in Columbia Women's Hospital, Washington, D.C., just after we moved to Riverdale. Angela was born October 10, 1963 at Holy Cross Hospital in Silver Spring, Maryland. The hospital was just opened, and Angie was one of the first babies delivered there. During the delivery the spinal bloc didn't work, and the surgeon kept cutting despite Mary Ellen screaming. They finally used gas to knock her out.

It was shortly after Angie was born. I was in graduate school. Mary Ellen was at home with six children a newborn,

1, 3, 4, 6, 7 years old. From November 1 to March 1, at least one of the children was sick every day. Needless to say, we were all exhausted. Finally, the doctor put the whole family on antibiotics. A month later Mary Ellen, still not recovered, went back to the doctor who said, "you have pneumonia, go home to bed." Six small children, husband in school (and teaching), and mother goes to bed? A neighbor, Mary Baldwin, with eight children of her own came over and cooked, cleaned, changed diapers, waited on Mary Ellen, and watched our children except when I was home. A week later when she was well, Mary Ellen asked our neighbor, "What can we ever do to repay you?" Her answer was "There is no way you can repay me, do it for someone else sometime." This type of neighborliness is more difficult in today's world where both parents are working full time.

When Angie was about 15 months old, she got sick which turned into pneumonia and the doctor put her into the hospital. He said we shouldn't visit but after a few days Mary Ellen couldn't wait and when she saw Angie so lethargic, she had a fit and demanded that the doctor do something. She went the next day and picked Angie up and they hugged and hugged. The doctor had Angie in a private room but moved her to a ward with other children. This may have helped Angie to perk up. After Angie was home, she kept getting up in the middle of the night and crawling in bed with us or one of her brothers or sisters. When we put her back to bed when she tried to sleep with us, she would return and sleep on the floor by our bed. This went on for quite some time.

Mary was very shy and sensitive. Once when we were out and Kenny was babysitting, he said no to her in a harsh voice. When we got home, we couldn't find her. We called and called, and everybody searched. Finally, we found her in the bathroom hiding between the bathtub and the sink cabinet.

Louie was born June 13, 1965 in Washington, D.C. and raised during the first 11 months at St. Ann's Home. St. Ann's told us that his mother was from Bolivia and his father a student from Turkey. Mary Ellen wanted more children but was unable to get pregnant again, so we decided to adopt. It was our good fortune that Louie was available for adoption through Catholic Charities. One look at his photo and we knew he was the one. He joined the family in May of 1966. Though Louie had been baptized at St. Ann's, we had a baptismal ceremony with Charles and Jerri Davis as godparents.

Unfortunately, our next-door neighbor, who was the local mailman, took it upon himself before we brought Louie home, to spread the word among the neighbors that "he was black." We received phone calls during the wee hours of the night with bomb threats and when Mary Ellen would push the stroller down the street people would peek out of their drapes. This was the height of the civil rights movement and parts of Maryland were very southern in attitudes. That neighbor later came over and said, "if I had known he was so light I wouldn't have said the things I did." I was so flabbergasted that all I could do was to yell, "get the hell out of here."

On the other hand, Charlie Davis, a friend and neighbor who was Louie's godfather, believed the neighborhood problems were rooted in the local Elks Club down the street that we were all members of because they had a swimming pool. He and I took Louie in the stroller to the club and Charlie sat him up on the bar and said, "do any of you s.o.b.s have a problem?" We were met with dead silence. That was the end of our local problems.

Mary Ellen and I joined the Catholic Interracial Council for Prince George County, eventually becoming the president couple and we ran into many of these racist attitudes. For example, the pastor of one parish in southern Prince George

County, that had separate altar rails for black and white parishioners said "we have no problems here" when we asked to hold a meeting in his church. Another time the auxiliary bishop of the Washington, D.C. diocese came to our parish in Riverdale and explained we needed to accept the fact that integration of the races was here and not going away. We didn't have to like it, but we best accept it. Hardly inspiring.

Friends of ours, who also were members of the Catholic Interracial Council, were African American and frequently faced the racism of the time. One was a chemist at Fort Meyer and owned property in the deep south. Whenever they had to travel there, they drove straight through because there were so few places to stay. She was quite light and talked about her brother "who passed" as white. He no longer could be in contact with his family for fear of being found out. They tried to get a $6,000 home improvement loan from our local bank and were turned down even though they had good income and property to put up as collateral. I went into the same bank and got a $6,000 personal loan with no collateral. The only difference; he was black, and I was white. I then loaned the funds to him.

On August 28, 1963, I joined with several hundred thousand other people to March on Washington. It was a time of great hope and expectations. We truly believed the song we sang: "We shall overcome, someday." When Dr. King spoke and said, "I have a dream...," it sent shivers down my back. We may have been naive, but we believed that dream was becoming a reality. Fifty years later it still is coming.

In 1964, after finishing all of my graduate studies except for the dissertation, I accepted a position teaching at The American University in Washington, D.C. This required a 45-minute commute each way. After the beltway opened, the time was reduced but the stress level from traffic increased. Teaching at American University was quite a change from Trinity College. It was a much larger school with a diverse student body, unlike the all-female prep atmosphere of Trinity. And at American I had graduate students, many of whom were older government workers. The student rebellions of the 1960s were just beginning, adding a whole new element to university life. More on this in the next chapter.

Speaking to a mostly white audience at Washington National Cathedral, March 31, 1968, Martin Luther King, Jr. said: "I don't like to predict violence...But if nothing is done between now and June to raise ghetto hope, I feel this summer will not only be as bad but worse than last year."[31] That previous summer, African Americans had rioted in cities across the country with 27 killed in Newark and 43 in Detroit.

Four days later, Thursday, April 4, 1968, Dr. King was assassinated in Memphis. The summer that followed was the worst ever. The Washington, D.C. riots of April 4–8, 1968, erupted with the assassination and, along with Chicago and Baltimore, was among the most affected.

At the busy intersection of 14th and U streets in Northwest DC—the heart of the District's black community—the news arrived on teenagers' transistor radios. People began to gather at the intersection, which was near the Washington office of King's Southern Christian Leadership Conference.

Stokely Carmichael—a Howard University graduate who would later become a nationally known Black Panther—led a group of young men into nearby businesses, demanding they shut down as they had when President Kennedy was killed in 1963. Carmichael urged people to remain calm, but the crowd grew.

Rioters, many of them teenagers, smashed windows, looted stores, and started fires. They tossed Molotov cocktails into buildings and threw bottles, bricks, and rocks at firefighters who tried to put out the blazes. The mood was part anger, part exhilaration. One of the owners of a restaurant in the area, and the only one that stayed open, said: "I remember the sadness more than anything else. The radio stations were playing hymns, and people were coming in crying... People were out of control with anger and sadness and frustration."[32]

On Friday, April 5, rioting spread to other sections of the District, especially Seventh Street in Northwest, H Street in Northeast, and parts of Anacostia. Federal troops and the National Guard were called in; they would number more than 13,600. Mayor Walter Washington ordered a 5:30 pm curfew. The riots continued on Saturday. Despite the chaos and demands from federal officials, Mayor Washington refused to order police to shoot rioters. The city smoldered on Sunday, but the worst was over. More than 800 fires had been started. Twelve people were dead and more than 1,000 injured. Rubble and charred buildings filled what had been vibrant neighborhoods.

On that Sunday, as the president couple of the Catholic Interracial Council in Prince George County, we received a request to bring food, medicines and clothing to the area at 14th and U streets. I along with three others loaded up food and other supplies collected from members plus bought at stores, and drove into the city. When we arrived at 14th and U, it was nothing but smoldering ruins. As we unloaded several shots rang out, whether aimed at us or not, I don't know. I do know we ducked down, hurriedly finished unloading, and got out of there.

Some weeks later, we got a phone call asking if we wanted to buy a new television. Mary Ellen, who had answered the phone, said no thanks. The caller then asked if we wanted to buy a new bicycle. Again, Mary Ellen said no, and she then asked the caller if these were from the riots. When the caller said yes, Mary Ellen said "we don't buy stolen stuff." The caller laughed and said, "that's stupid."

Our time in Riverdale was coming to an end. Our family had grown by three, we had fought through the bigotry in the neighborhood, I had finished my PhD at Maryland, and found a new job, moving from Trinity College to The American University.

Later in the summer of 1968 we moved into the northwest section of D.C. just as many were leaving the city for the suburbs. Reducing my commute time was key but also being closer to friends and colleagues from the university was important.

# CHAPTER VI

## Graduate School and Development Economics

*We can cure physical diseases with medicine,*
*but the only cure for loneliness, despair, and hopelessness is love.*
*There are many in the world who are dying for a piece of bread*
*but there are many more dying for a little love.*

—MOTHER TERESA, *A Simple Path*

WITH THE THEOLOGICAL and philosophical background, I obtained from my CFM work in Oregon and my experiences in Puerto Rico, I was drawn into graduate work in economics by my desire to attain a better understanding of the causes of poverty and how to overcome it. Msgr. Ivan Illich had convinced me that I needed to get a Ph.D. in economics before anyone would listen to what I had to say. Thus, I accepted an assistantship at the University of Maryland with the intention of concentrating on the problems of development in Third World countries.

At that time the economics department at Maryland was dominated by Keynesians and even included courses in Institutionalism. However, they were all thoroughgoing secularists. As a Christian I wanted more. Two sources led me to see how my faith and the economics I was learning could be reinforcing. The early 1960s issues of *The Review of Social Economy* are where I found many articles that connected economics and my Catholic faith. Articles critiquing the economic man idea in light of faith forced me to think creatively.[33] Other articles on Joseph Schumpeter's approach opened new ways of seeing the economy in a more dynamic model.

A second important source for seeing connections between faith and economics was in the History of Economic Thought class I was required to take where we actually read Adam Smith's the *Wealth of Nations*[34] and the *Theory of Moral Sentiments*.[35] Doing so was a revelation. At that time most mainstream economists saw themselves following in his footsteps. However, I found that Smith had much in common with CST. I came to see that the popular version of Smith's theory that the so-called invisible hand of the free market converts the self-interest of individuals into the maximum social good is a caricature of the real Adam Smith. I have come to a fuller understanding of my original impressions through the work of others, particularly that of Professor Jerry Evensky.[36]

Smith's writings, especially his *Theory of Moral Sentiments*, suggest that he had a much more nuanced understanding of human beings than the one which assumes that individuals are driven solely by self-interest. Although Smith argued that self-interest has a strong influence on people's behavior, he had a pluralist view of human nature, in which empathy—the ability to perceive things from another person's perspective—also has an important role.

Moreover, his views on the role of self-interest leading to the common good are not so clear cut either. He thought that "humanity, justice, generosity, and public spirit, are the qualities most useful to others,"[37] and believed that while self-interest is useful in certain situations, these virtues are useful in other cases.

Especially towards the end of his life Smith began to have doubts about the role of the invisible hand of competition and self interest in yielding the common good. In his revision of the *Theory of Moral Sentiments* in 1789, he added a new sixth part containing a practical system of morality. He appeals to all people to place the well-being of society as a whole above that of their own factions, and stresses especially the role of statesmen in constructing such a moral society through their actions and by setting examples for others.

For Adam Smith virtue serves as "the fine polish to the wheels of society" while vice is "like the vile rust, which makes them jar and grate upon one another."[38] So Adam Smith would be quite comfortable reading in *Laudato Si*, [LS, 109, 123] Pope Francis's statement that: "The economy accepts every advance in technology with a view to profit, without concern for its potentially negative impact on human beings. ... Yet by itself the market cannot guarantee integral human development and social inclusion."[39] Rather we are called to control the unrestricted pursuit of profit by allowing ethics to guide us as citizens and consumers so that both the planet and all peoples can thrive.

The early 1960s, when I was in graduate school, appeared to be a propitious time for a Christian to be studying economics. Development economics was born after World War II with the acceptance of the inevitability of political, social, and economic change. The problems of the poor countries of Southeastern Europe were the genesis of much of the initial work, and then the success in rebuilding Europe and Japan emboldened development economists to extend their work to the rest of the world. The break-up of the English and French colonial empires added further emphasis to issues of overcoming poverty. The growing cold war between the United States and its allies against the Soviet Union and its allies helped focus development attention on strategic areas of the so-called Third World. Development thought incorporated an optimism that change could be for the better and that conscious reflection on and control over change, often through national governments and international organizations, could harness change and bring about development.

Thus, the 1950s and 1960s were marked by optimism that world poverty could be conquered by economic growth. Since economists assumed that the question of the nature of a good society was already answered, the issue became one of solving certain practical problems. The good society was simply assumed to be an idealized version of the United States economy, that is, a market economy driven by a consumerist society. The key to a consumer society was growth of per capita income. Thus, the vast bulk of the development literature focused on economic growth rates as the *deus ex machina* to solve all problems.

My own focus on development issues got channeled through a complex set of circumstances. First was the language requirement for the PhD. Two languages, French and German, were required with the option of substituting for one language by a third needed for your dissertation. Substituting Spanish for French was a no-brainer since I knew the former and not the latter. However, that meant I had to pass an exam in German. The exam consisted in translating a page from a book by Werner Sombart, a 19th century economist. The exam was timed, no dictionary, and the page not known in advance. As I begin to study German it became clear that no way I was going to master this in any reasonable time horizon. Thus, Plan B became one of prepping my high school Russian and studying for the French exam. I passed the Russian exam easily, but the French went on the back burner while I focused on getting a dissertation topic. The department also required several areas for comprehensive examinations. Beyond the required theory fields, I chose economic development and comparative economic systems. Given my Russian, it made sense to take courses on the Russian economy, history, and geography. Given these two specialties, my dissertation topic, *The Soviet Model of Economic Development*,[40] was a natural outcome.

I finished my course work and exams at the end of the Spring semester of 1964. As noted earlier, I then accepted a regular position at The American University in Washington, D.C. and quit the one at Trinity College. I finished the dissertation in 1966. During this period, 1962-66, I struggled to find an approach to economic development that I could fully accept. I found the mainstream approach to be unrealistic from my experience in Puerto Rico. A number of my fellow graduate students were heavily into studying Marxian economics in informal study groups. It was appealing at first, but the focus on class conflict as the driving force of history struck me as overblown. Also, a key aspect of Jesus's teaching is we are to love our enemies. Needless to say, I eventually became marginal to the group.

I continued to work on development issues for the next 30 years.[41] In the 1970s the hope that underdevelopment would be soon conquered was dashed by growing unemployment and inequality and the intractability of absolute poverty. However, the 1970s also witnessed the birth of a new optimism to replace the old. The pursuit of "growth with equity" or a strategy of targeting "basic human needs" would succeed where economic growth failed.

The 1980s ushered in a period of greater caution. It became widely recognized that world poverty would not be eliminated with simple economic panaceas. Resource shortages (particularly of energy), environmental destruction, rising protectionism in the industrial world, militarism in the Third World, the international arms race, the structure of the world economy all made the design of development strategies a complex problem in political economy rather than a simple technical economic issue.

By the end of the 1990s the Washington Consensus[42] of free markets and free trade begin to fall apart. Economists became more aware of the problems created by fast economic growth and slow social change, as well as the difficulty of defining development correctly. Development economics had to learn that "all good things do not go together," that rapid growth and economic development may be accompanied by severe social and political problems such as the loss of deeply felt cultural values, the breakup of community, and the emergence of authoritarian governments.

It is now into the second decade of the twenty first century, a time when the old verities are collapsing. The rise of the BRICs—Brazil, Russia, India, China—using a wide variety of development approaches dominates development discussions. The cold war is a distant memory, the Eastern European countries have moved from centrally planned economies of the Soviet type to market-oriented countries. Regional and ethnic conflicts have moved to center stage in the international political arena with the most notable examples being the wars in Iraq, Syria, Afghanistan, the internal conflicts in much of the middle east, in Somalia, Rwanda, much of central Africa.

Despite all this, much has been accomplished since 1945. There has been rapid growth of GDP throughout the world, infant mortality has decreased dramatically, and life expectancy has increased rapidly; and access to education has been extended far beyond what would have been imaginable in 1945.

Unfortunately, at the heart of this consumerist and profit-driven economic development philosophy is a wrong-footed idea of dominion. The result is exploitation, and a throwaway attitude towards nature, culture, and human life itself. Pope Francis, in his encyclical *Laudato Si*, calls for a bold cultural revolution in our attitude to development and progress. He puts it rather bluntly: "Nobody is suggesting a return to the Stone Age, but we do need to slow down and look at reality in a different way, to appropriate the positive and sustainable progress which has been made, but also to recover the values and the great goals swept away by our unrestrained delusions of grandeur." [para. 114]

There are scholars in whose perspective, culture is seen as a vital and, sometimes, revered aspect of a people's identity, and as representing the integral and holistic nature of a society that changes in response to internal and external pressures. Culture is not apart from or outside of economic life but is instead integral to and interactive with it.

A close friend and well-known Catholic scholar of this view was Denis Goulet,[43] who advocated an understanding of development that respected local cultures while at the same time recognizing the need for cultures to change. Goulet thus tried to find a way out of what he termed *'The Cruel Choice,'* which forced cultures outside the Western mainstream to choose between keeping their local cultural traditions and staying poor or opting to join modernizing trends and losing their identity and sense of meaning.[44] His solution was to work within cultures and to find the 'latent dynamisms' that allowed cultural groups to respond constructively to the challenges of modernization.

While there are several reasons to be concerned with the ethics of the development process, there are three that have become prominent in CST. First, while it is recognized that development helps people by creating jobs, excessive consumption by some individuals and nations while at the same time other individuals and nations suffer from hunger and sickness, is judged morally unacceptable. Income spent on luxuries could have been made available to others for their necessities. Typical is Pope Paul VI's statement: "...the superfluous wealth of rich countries should be placed at the service of poor nations...Otherwise their continued greed will certainly call down upon them the judgment of God and the wrath of the poor..." [PP, para. 49] The related problem of consumption spending on products produced under sweatshop conditions is recognized as a serious problem for the rights of workers and the obligations of employers.

Second, excessive development which threatens the earth's environment is morally condemned. Pope John Paul II stated: "Equally worrying is the ecological question which accompanies the problem of consumerism and which is closely connected to it. In his desire to have and to enjoy rather than to be and to grow, man consumes the resources of the earth and his own life in an excessive and distorted way." [CA, para. 37] Pope Francis's encyclical, Laudato Si, as quoted at the beginning of this chapter, begins with an "urgent challenge to protect our common home...to bring the whole human family together to seek a sustainable and integral development, for we know that things can change" [para. 13]. Pope Francis calls the earth our "common home," which is like our sister and our mother. But we are damaging this familial relationship as we harm the environment. In so doing, we are damaging our relationship with other humans, particularly those least equipped to defend themselves: the poor and future generations. We are forgetting our interconnectedness with the earth and with all the people in the world now and the generations to come who depend on our good stewardship of the gift of creation. The encyclical firmly posits that a truly ecological approach is also inherently social—an approach that simultaneously hears the cry of the earth and the cry of the poor.

Third, treating consumption as the primary goal of development—that is, focusing on *having* instead of *being*—is detrimental to human dignity. It is this third concern that I will expand on here.

The Catholic tradition condemns the materialist view of human welfare. In his 1968 encyclical, *Populorum Progressio*, Pope Paul VI wrote:

> Increased possession is not the ultimate goal of nations or of individuals. All growth is ambivalent. It is essential if man is to develop as a man, but in a way it imprisons man if he considers it the supreme good, and it restricts his vision. Then we see hearts harden and minds close, and men no longer gather together in friendship but out of self-interest, which soon leads to oppositions and disunity. The exclusive pursuit of possessions thus becomes an obstacle to individual fulfillment and to man's true greatness. Both for nations and for individual men, avarice is the most evident form of moral underdevelopment. [para. 19]

On the twentieth anniversary (1987) of *Populorum Progressio*, Pope John Paul II wrote in Sollicitudo Rei Socialis: "All of us experience firsthand the sad effects of this blind submission to pure consumerism: in the first place a crass materialism, and at the same time a radical dissatisfaction because one quickly learns...that the more one possesses the more one wants, while deeper aspirations remain unsatisfied and perhaps even stifled." [Para. 28] In his later social encyclical—*Centesimus Annus*[1992]—marking the one hundredth anniversary of *Rerum Novarum,* Pope John Paul II writes: "It is not wrong to want to live better; what is wrong is a style of life which is presumed to be better when it is directed toward 'having' rather than 'being,' and which wants to have more, not in order to be more but in order to spend life in enjoyment as an end in itself." [para. 36]

He also argues that there must be social intervention on the international level. To carry out this effort, "it is not enough to draw on the surplus goods which in fact our world abundantly produces: it requires above all a change of life-styles, of models of production and consumption, and of the established structures of power which today govern societies." [CA, 58] This strikes at the very heart of a consumption-oriented market system.

Pope Francis has continued and expanded this concern with the development of poor countries. He says in an address during an *Audience with the participants in the Convention organized by the Dicastery for Promoting Integral Human Development on the fiftieth anniversary of "Populorum Progressio"* (2018): "What does full or integral development mean… It means *integrating the different peoples of the earth.* The duty of solidarity requires us to seek fair ways of sharing, so that there is no longer that dramatic inequality between those who have too much and those who have nothing, between those who discard and those who are discarded. Only the path of integration between peoples can permit to humanity a future of peace and hope."[45]

## My Field Experience in Development

I need to leaven the preceding discussion of CST on development and the succeeding section on economic theory with thoughts on my field experiences with development in British Honduras (now Belize), Chile, and Peru.

***British Honduras****.* During the summer of 1962 I was in charge of creating a training program focused on the history and culture of two South American countries—Venezuela and

British Honduras. This was designed to prepare Peace Corps volunteers to work in those countries. This was only the second year that the Peace Corps existed so there were many snafus and inefficiencies. The University of Maryland was chosen to house this summer training program and the faculty director chose me to actually set up and run the program. I had just finished one year of graduate school so they must have been hard up for someone with experience. Further complicating things, at the last minute they added Turkey to our list of countries. Thank heavens, language skills were taught elsewhere. I recruited experts in the history and culture of each country from the local universities and the State Department.

Since we could find no one who knew much about British Honduras, I was sent there for three weeks to learn about the places the volunteers would be serving. There were 43 volunteers and all but three were going to be teachers in local schools. The other three would be working as marine biologists in the fishing industry. British Honduras had no public-school system, rather all the schools were run by the St. Louis Province of Jesuits. The language was English, and the curriculum was based on the one used in England. Few made it past the A level exams and fewer still into college of which there were none in British Honduras. The country was so little developed that most roads began and ended in Belize City, the capital. Thus, I traveled the country visiting the schools via Jeep on what passed for roads, and motorboats on the rivers. Agriculture was not well developed except for peanut farming. One day in the back country we came across a horse-drawn buggy with a family, white skinned, clothed all in black. It turned out that Amish settlers from Ohio in the 1850s dominated the peanut farms. I had dinner with the British Counsel, and he showed little interest in economic development of the country. I had similar reactions from some of the priests I interviewed at the schools. One said: "Don't send me any of those radical Kennedy types." Clearly, since those days, British Honduras, now Belize, has chosen to focus on tourism as the road to development. This is not surprising, in 1962 the total population was 90,000 giving a working population of around 30,000. This small of a labor force could not support a wide range of industry.

*Chile*. In the early 1970s, the Department of Economics at The American University joined with the Inter-American Development Bank to create a M.A. degree program in development banking. Needing to recruit a first class of students, I went to Columbia, Bolivia, and Chile to interview potential graduate students. Most of them were already working in the Inter-American Development Bank or similar institutions.

While in Chile I pursued my own research agenda by interviewing various government economic ministers. My interest was on how the socialist regime of President Allende was going to operate in what was an overwhelmingly capitalist economy. I asked why would business owners accept all the restrictions and takeovers that were being suggested? Their answer was always: Chileans are different! Obviously, they turned out to be wrong with the General Pinochet coup.

*Peru.* In 1984 I was contacted by the Catholic religious order of priests, Oblates of Mary Immaculate (OMI). The order is divided into regional provinces around the world. The Latin America province argued that the main cause of poverty and underdevelopment there was United States imperialism and they wanted the United States province to publicly state the same. The Canadian province agreed with the Latin Americans and the result was constant wrangling in their provincial meetings. They decided, therefore, to hold a joint meeting for

10 days in March 1985, outside Lima, Peru. Each province was to choose a technical adviser for the meeting.

The United States province asked me to be their adviser. I was to provide a week-long seminar on economic development to their delegates to the March meeting. The seminar was held in Washington, D.C. and focused on issues of development and economic relation between the United States and the Latin American countries.

I then accompanied the United States delegation to the retreat center. Each of the technical advisers made presentations, both singly and jointly in panels, while advising their delegates during discussion sessions. While no unanimous decision was reached, they did produce a 30 minute video that highlighted the issues for those back in each of the provinces.

## Toward a New Economics

From 1964 to 1975 I was on the faculty at The American University. Since 1975 I have been at the University of Notre Dame. During this time, I became ever more disenchanted with traditional economic theory as the vehicle to develop adequate policies to overcome poverty in the Third World or in the United States. I found myself unable to accept the values embedded in economic theory, particularly the elevation of self-interest because it supposedly leads to efficiency, the neglect of income distribution, and the attempts to export these values into studies of the family, the role of the state and so on. Both Christian thought and biblical tradition make self-interest a central aspect of *fallen* human nature which as Christian believers we are bound to strive to counter with prayer, good works, and the cultivation of virtue.

How has CST impacted my view of economics as a means of correcting social problems in the world? My whole life I have grappled with the question: "Was the Good Samaritan a bad economist?" In Charles Dickens' novel, *Hard Times*, his character Thomas Gradgrind is: "A man of realities. A man of facts and calculations. A man who proceeds upon the principle that two and two are four, and nothing over, and who is not to be talked into allowing for anything over."[46] Thus, he "sat writing in the room with the deadly statistical clock, proving something no doubt—probably, in the main, that the Good Samaritan was a Bad Economist."[47]

"'Some persons hold,' he pursued, still hesitating, 'that there is a wisdom of the Head, and that there is a wisdom of the Heart. I have not supposed so; but, as I have said, I mistrust myself now. I have supposed the head to be all-sufficient. It may not be all-sufficient...'"[48]

What is that wisdom of the heart and where is it found; certainly not in economics alone? To use Isaiah Berlin's words, we need to be foxes not hedgehogs.[49] Hedgehogs distill the world's complexity into a simple and universal theory. Foxes do the opposite and are skeptical of simple theories about complex systems such as national economies. I believe Economics needs the humanities, particularly theology and religious belief, to be the fox that makes their theories more realistic and more humane.

Morton Schapiro, professor of economics and president of Northwestern University highlights the limitations of economic theory by reflecting on his experiences of working in Egypt to "get prices right" in the 1980s. Under pressure from many economists and international agencies, the Egyptian government felt compelled to end their subsidies on bread and other goods for the poor. This allowed these goods to rise to market clearing levels, substantially higher than they were before. "Sitting with a 'thrilled' group of economists, Schapiro was haunted by reports indicating that this policy lead to riots, malnutrition, and death. Were these policies nevertheless justified? How does one properly weigh the value of life and death?"[50] This same issue dominates political, economic, and ethical discussions in the current year of 2020. What is the trade-off between personal freedoms and loss of life from opening up the economy during the coronavirus?

Let me give one more example about the head wisdom of economics and the lack of wisdom of the heart: "...onchocerciasis, also known as river blindness... is a parasitic disease that has cost millions of people their eyesight, and is endemic in large parts of sub-Saharan Africa. In 1974, seven West African nations got together, contacted donors, and set out to create the Onchocerciasis Control Program, overseen by the World Health Organization. The program was a huge success, in that it prevented hundreds of thousands of people from going blind, but there was a problem: the economists involved couldn't show that the venture was worth it. A cost-benefit analysis was "inconclusive": the people who were being helped were so poor that the benefit of saving their eyesight didn't have much monetary impact. 'There are humanitarian benefits associated with reducing the blindness and suffering caused by onchocerciasis,' the World Bank report allowed. But 'these benefits are inherently unmeasurable, and we will not account for them here.' In other words, the very thing that made the project so admirable—that it was improving the lives of the poorest people in the world—also made it, from an economic point of view, not really worth doing."[51]

In my career as an economist, I have tried to be the fox that brings wisdom of the heart to economics. That is, the social science of economics needs to be leavened with the heart wisdom of the humanities including theology and religious faith. How do the humanities differ from economics as a social science?

Economists tend to be hedgehogs, forever on the search for a single, unifying explanation of complex phenomena. They take large, complicated issues involving human behavior and reduce it to an equation: supply-and-demand curves; the Phillips curve, which shows the relation between unemployment and inflation; or GDP, which measures total production and how rich we all are.

Economics has three systematic biases: "it ignores the role of culture, it ignores the fact that "to understand people one must tell stories about them," and it constantly touches on ethical questions beyond its ken. Culture, stories, and ethics are things that can't be reduced to equations, and economics accordingly has difficulty with them."[52] This is where the fox-like approach of the humanities is needed.

The humanist approach is *holistic*. It is always concerned not only with a person's relationship to themselves but also their relationship with others, to social institutions, the physical world, God, history, as well as the economy itself. The obverse is also true: to the humanistic mind, things, incidents, even words are meaningless in isolation. Meaning is a function of tone, gesture, and situation as well as the denotation of words.

The humanist mind believes in *mystery*. It believes in the unexpected, the unpredictable, the uncontrollable, the un-knowable. It believes in that which is beyond logic, that which is too complex for rational understanding. It doubts the basic Aristotelian premise that "a" cannot be both "a" and "not-a." The process of reconciling opposites is indeed fundamental. Ambiguity, irony, paradox are essential categories. They do not represent challenges to be overcome so much as realities to be discovered and revealed.

The humanist mind analyzes life by *esthetic reasoning*. Basic to its forms of thought is a thinking process by which conflict and contradiction are discovered in unity, and unity is revealed in contradiction.

The humanistic mind believes in *subjectivity*. It takes emotions seriously. It believes as much in knowing experientially what it feels like to hold a certain conviction as in knowing rationally an idea's logical implications or practical consequences. It believes that a person is more than the sum of his/her behavior, age, sex, socio-economic status, etc. It does not deny their importance but believes there must be room for intuition and insight; and, I might add, room for God's grace. Writing in the Fourth Century, Macarius of Egypt, an Egyptian Christian monk and hermit said:

> *The heart itself is but a small vessel,*
> *yet dragons are there, and there are also lions;*
> *there are poisonous beasts and all the treasures of evil.*
> *But there too is God,*
> *the angels,*
> *the life and the kingdom,*
> *the light and the apostles,*
> *the heavenly cities and the treasures of grace—*
> *all things are there.*

The humanist is concerned with the *concrete*. It imagines how an individual will behave under a particular set of circumstances. It approaches understanding by narrating about one person rather than generalizing about many, by metaphor rather than by principle. Its interest in abstractions is less in their truth or logic than in how people act who believe them. Like a golfer, the humanist succeeds not by memorizing rules but by imagining the precise line the ball must follow to land in the cup.

The humanist mind tends to be *apocalyptic*. It is concerned with first things and last and with such ultimate states of being as life, death, and freedom. Loss, suffering, failure, defeat are not merely unsolved problems, but part of the ultimate comedy/tragedy called life. A poor, homeless, unwed mother is more than a symbol for social reform; she, too, is a child of God. Solutions to social problems as often involve changes in human perception as they do changes in external conditions.

I have tried over the years to get the fox and the hedgehog to work together in my writings. As a result, I started researching and writing on the philosophy of science as it applied to economics. This work led me to two important conclusions. First is the conviction that economic theory is not value free as is so often claimed, but rather, it presupposes a set of value judgments upon which economic analysis is erected. Second is the realization that the economy itself requires that the self-interest of economic actors be morally constrained

Over time I came to see myself as a social economist that questioned the free market model with its emphasis on fulfilling consumer preferences as the primary criterion of human welfare and as the engine of economic growth and development. The fundamental premises of this social economics, in contrast to mainstream economics, and complementary to CST are fourfold:

First, economic actors as persons are the basic unit of the economy. Second, they act freely but within certain limits, self-interestedly but often with regard for others, and calculatedly but at times impulsively, whimsically, or altruistically, in a self-regulating economy which from time to time must be constrained deliberately in order to serve the common good[53] and to protect the weak and the needy. Third, their economic behavior is grounded in reason and in faith,[54] changing as economic conditions change but at times reflecting moral rules and principles, predictable and unforeseeable, and knowable with mathematical certainty and empirical precision but sometimes mysterious and beyond human understanding. Fourth, their worth at times may be construed instrumentally but finally is not reducible to economic calculus because it rests squarely on the conviction that humans have a worth and dignity beyond measure.[55]

These premises explain why social economists like me see the economic world differently and approach policy questions differently than mainstream economics. To social economists:

> ...economic acts are both moral and economic. They are economic in that they are necessary means for persons to act and survive. At the same time the acts are moral or immoral insofar as they relate to dealing justly with other people and in using material things as means to their ultimate good and purpose. Thus economics is both a praxis and a science... As a science it...may be correct or incorrect but not morally right or wrong. As a praxis, however, ...economic acts or economic conduct... can also be judged unjust, imprudent, intemperate, and in general moral or immoral.[56]

Instead of the neo-classical *homo economicus*, social economists focus on the whole person, sometimes labeled *homo socio-economics*.[57] This enables us to utilize concepts usually excluded from mainstream economics: needs, power, equity, gender, culture, family, institutional context, among others. This focus requires social economists to incorporate value frameworks that include the use of terms such as fairness, human dignity, human rights, and the common good.

Clearly the view of human behavior in social economics is much richer than in mainstream economics but that very richness of detail causes problems for economic research and policy making. The power of the economic model is that its simplicity lends itself to formal modeling and empirical research in a way impossible for the more complex models of social economics. But is there really an advantage?

## Modernization vs Convoluted Development

The collapse of the Washington Consensus has opened the debate on best approaches to development. No longer do the prescriptions of free market economists hold sway without question. More and more policy proposals on development issues recognize the problems of consumerism, sustainability, and human dignity posed by social economists.

As with CST, for social economists, economics and ethics are inherently intertwined.[58] Development ethics, as espoused by social economists, is closely connected with the meaning of development as integral human development. This section briefly examines the main themes of development ethics that are found in the writings of social economists working on development problems.[59]

First, social economists are concerned not so much with economic growth per se but with the increase in the material wellbeing of the poor. But they go beyond that. For instance, they engage in ethical discussions of why one should care about the poor. Goulet, for example, argues that individuals, groups and nations who are better off have obligations to those who are worse off, calling this "solidarity". One can provide religious and philosophical justifications of absolute respect for the dignity of the human person, regardless of gender, ethnic group, social class, religion, age or nationality. But Goulet also argues that such obligations follow from some empirical realities; that is, the fact that the rich and poor are involved in one socio-economic unity and that the activities of one group have important effects on the other. For this reason, all groups have a responsibility towards others. Since the rich arguably have a larger influence, they may be held to be especially responsible for the poor. These concerns are relevant not only within countries but also between countries, especially in the context of globalization.[60]

Second, there is a stress on the environment, not only because of the contribution that it makes to material well-being—

an issue which is often stressed by mainstream economists and that was mentioned above—but mainly because of its intrinsic importance. There is a recognition of the relation of human beings with nature, facilitating responsible use, respectful of biological cycles and the equilibrium of ecosystems - especially those of tropical forests—and in solidarity with future generations.

Third, development is much more than material well-being. It incorporates other changes including, particularly, that of values. Goulet[61] has argued forcefully that development is fundamentally a question of human values and attitudes, goals defined by societies for themselves, and criteria for determining what tolerable costs are to be borne, and by whom, in the course of change. Modernization is not the goal if it is imposed from outside, especially if it destroys values that are of central importance to those who are experiencing development. Social economists also acknowledge the problems of over-consumption. Material goods, of food, housing, medicine, and security, are important because they contribute something essential to human well-being. They also argue against ever-increasing consumption of material goods and consumerism, where the focus is on "having" and not "being."[62] While for many people this view of materialism and consumerism has religious overtones, recent research on subjective well-being also points out that beyond a certain level of income and consumption further increases do not add significantly, or sometimes not at all, to increases in happiness (See further discussion in the section on globalization below).

Fourth, if development is recognized as a means to an end, what is it a means to and how do we find out these ends? Social economists go well beyond the technical focus of much of the literature on the meaning of development by proposing ways in which one can select and weight different ends so they can be included in the concept of development. Some, such as Goulet, focus on religious traditions because of the major hold they have on many societies, but argue for an enlightened and critical borrowing of these traditions such as that espoused by Mahatma Gandhi rather than a fundamentalist one. More importantly, they recommend that development scholars and practitioners examine what people in developing societies, especially the poor who are not trapped by vested interests, want. They argue that authentic development occurs only when people themselves decide what they mean by development.[64]

Not only do mainstream economists and social economists have different views of human nature and the role of ethics but they work out of different conceptions of history—one of historical progress versus one less deterministic, more convoluted.

How does the historical experience of the rise of capitalist economies in the now developed world impact the theory and practice of development today? Mainstream views of development continue to follow in the Modernization tradition that arose in the aftermath of WW II. On this view the primary measure of development continues to be a self-reinforcing tendency to economic growth and material progress. It is from this basic developmental reality that other positive features of a good society spring, like better health care, improved education and democratic governance. Over time it has become clear that an equitably growing economy requires financial capital, the adoption of efficient technologies, investment, human capital, entrepreneurship and market promoting policies and institutions, which begs the question of how to get nations to build and use these necessary attributes.

The social economists' concept of convoluted history is that there is no simple historical march of progress. There are no general paths to development just as there is no general definition of development. Each people must write its own history. As Denis Goulet says regarding the strategy of development pursued by Guinea-Bissau: "Paradoxically, the lesson of greatest importance is that *the best model of development is the one that any society forges for itself on the anvil of its own specific conditions.*"

What does this mean for the development economist? There is an interesting parallel in modern medicine in a tension between the "scientific" explanation of a disease and the diagnosis a clinician makes for a particular patient. This is well described by Tolstoy in *War and Peace:*

> Doctors came to see Natasha, both separately and in consultation. They said a great deal in French, German and in Latin. They criticised one another, and prescribed the most diverse remedies for all the diseases they were familiar with. But it never occurred to one of them to make the simple reflection that they could not understand the disease from which Natasha was suffering, as no single disease can be fully understood in a living person; for every living person has his complaints unknown to medicine—not a disease of the lungs, of the kidneys, of the skin, of the heart, and so on, as described in medical books, but a disease that consists of one out of the innumerable combinations of ailments of these organs.[65]

While Tolstoy's depiction of every illness as a unique event may no longer be justified, economic development is even more of an art than medical diagnosis. Economic theorists can scientifically explain the results of underpricing capital regardless of country or time. Development economists, on the other hand, are diagnosticians of the particular illnesses of particular countries at specific points in time. They are forced to transcend a specific scientific paradigm to become artisans of the particular. They are foxes not hedgehogs.

An adequate agenda of domestic and international economic policies requires good intentions, clear analysis of the issues, and sustained carry through. All are in short supply in an international economy driven by self-interest, both personal and national. The present style of globalization threatens to generate a whirlwind of political backlash. We need to heed the warning given by James Weaver,[66] economist, Church of Christ minister, and social activist, in a talk entitled "Globalization with a Human Face:"[67]

*I have wondered about which human face represents the globalization system of the future. There are many candidates. One can see the face of John Maynard Keynes at Bretton Woods, NH in 1944 working to create a new international political economic order that would prevent another Great Depression and world war. One can see the face of a woman in Vietnam who has gotten a job in a Nike shoe factory. One can see the face of Jody Williams and the NGO's, who got most nations in the world to sign a treaty to ban the use of land mines. One can see the face of an auto worker protesting in Seattle because he lost his job when his factory relocated to Mexico. One can see the face of an AIDs patient in South Africa. One can see the face of Osama bin Ladin. (Or in 2020 the face of ISIS!)*

# CHAPTER VII

# Washington, D.C.: Family as a Mediating Institution

*With what care, human kindness and justice do I conduct myself at work?*
*How will my economic decisions to buy, sell, invest, divest, hire,*
*or fire serve human dignity and the common good?*
*In what career can I best exercise my talents so as to fill the world*
*with the Spirit of Christ?*
*How do my economic choices contribute to the strength of my family*
*and community, to the values of my children, to a sensitivity to those in need?*
*In this consumer society, how can I develop a healthy detachment*
*from things and avoid the temptation to assess who I am by what I have?*
*How do I strike a balance between labor and leisure that enlarges*
*my capacity for friendships, for family life, for community?*
*What government policies should I support to attain the well-being of all,*
*especially the poor and vulnerable?*

—ECONOMIC JUSTICE FOR ALL, PASTORAL MESSAGE [ Para. 23]

IN AUGUST 1968 we moved to NW 30th Street in Washington, DC. It was a lovely brick house with four bedrooms on the 2nd floor and a large bedroom on the 3rd floor. It had a finished basement with half bath and knotty pine paneling that later we remodeled part of into another bedroom. There were two bathrooms on the 2nd floor and a half bath on the main floor along with a living room, dining room, eat-in kitchen, and den. There was a small fenced in back yard and a screened in front porch.

A week after we moved to the new house, our friends the Firths called to say their house had burned and could they stay with us. They stayed a month. All told we were 19 people. No one complained about doubling up in single beds, sleeping on the floor, or having no privacy. I was gone during part of the time doing research in London. Thus, the burden fell primarily on Mary Ellen, who bore it with her usual efficiency and equinimity. She said, "Well, that gives us an extra sleeping space." She moved into a single bed giving Hans and Madeline our double bed.

Before moving, Kenny, Teresa, Matt and Alice attended St. Bernard's school in Riverdale. After moving, we switched them to Blessed Sacrament school except for Kenny because they were not admitting new 7th or 8th graders. We enrolled him into St. Alban's where he had to wear a coat and tie. At his request his mom sewed him a bright orange sport jacket. He made a splash at the school with his sport jacket and his prayer of the faithful after the 1968 presidential elections, "May God forgive the American people for electing Richard Nixon."

We lived on 30th street from August 1968 until August 1975 when we left for South Bend, Indiana and a new position for me at the University of Notre Dame. The neighborhood on 30th street was special. We made life-long friends like Jerry & Joy Choppin and David & Rose Ederer, both CFM couples. Our children had tons of playmates up and down the street and on the adjoining ones, and we even had block parties, with the street blocked off, in this huge city. It was a real neighborhood, a true community.

Let me give two examples of this sense of community, one small and one large. In 1975 when we had our house up for sale a potential buyer was looking at it when they asked whether that was a goat they heard braying. In fact, the Choppin's across the street had a goat in their back yard. Mary Ellen responded saying, "Yes and if that bothers you, you don't belong in this neighborhood."

On a more serious level, in 1972, neighbors down the street had been recently convicted of embezzling $90,000 from their employer, Liberty Lobby. They failed to show up for sentencing and the wife and children were arrested at a street corner while delivering newspapers. The husband was picked up later that day. The mother said, "children, go to the Wilber's." Seven children, ages 2 to 13, arrived at our door saying, "Mom says stay here." If we didn't take them, they would be sent to a notorious children's center where beatings and molestations were an everyday occurrence. A day later two police officers and one person from the welfare department came to the house. They said, "we have come to take the children." "You are not taking them anywhere" Mary Ellen replied. "You are willing to take care of them?" they said. She replied yes. "Fine, thank you, goodbye" they said!

We were in a wonderful CFM group at the time. We got together and agreed to take the children until the parents were out of jail. The Choppin's took two of the children, four other families took one each, and we kept Frankie who was six. Almost two years later the children returned to their parents upon completion of their jail sentences.

Frankie lived with us for two years. He was younger than Louie but bigger physically. They shared a bedroom and played together. He was a tough little guy when we got him. At five he would go by himself on the public bus to a swimming pool in Georgetown. When Mary Ellen tried to take a book of matches away from him, he cursed her out. Slowly he opened up and became a regular member of the family. We were sad to see him return to his dysfunctional family after the parents got out of jail.

Ever since our time in the Beaverton CFM group we have striven as a family to make our faith reach out to others in need. Our CFM group in Washington and the community on 30th street reinforced us in doing so.

It was during these years that I began to more fully understand the importance of the concept of subsidiarity, that is foundational in CST. David Brooks, columnist for the New York Times writes: "A society is healthy when its culture counterbalances its economics. That is to say, when you have a capitalist economic system that emphasizes competition, dynamism and individual self-interest, you need a culture that celebrates cooperation, stability and committed relationships. We don't have that. We have a culture that takes the disruptive and dehumanizing aspects of capitalism and makes them worse."[68] He concludes with a statement that "The lone wolf man has had his day; the weaving man is what we need, the one strong enough to bind himself into a community."[69] The problem is that those communities, what I call mediating institutions, such as the family, the church, the neighborhood are all in decline.

CST sees society as made up of a dense network of relations among individuals, families, churches, neighborhood associations, business firms, labor unions, and different levels of government. Thus, every level of society has a role to play in ensuring basic human rights and the common good. This is expressed as the "principle of subsidiarity:" This principle provides for a pluralism of social actors. Each, from the individual person to the federal government, has obligations. Higher levels should not usurp the authority of lower levels except when necessary. Here, I want to focus on the family and its role in society as a mediating institution.

Our modern political philosophies—liberalism, conservatism, socialism—have failed precisely because they have not understood the importance of mediating institutions such as the family. Liberalism has constantly turned to the state and conservatism to the market and corporate sector for solutions to social problems. Neither recognizes the destructiveness to the social fabric caused by relying on mega institutions. Socialism also suffers from this myopia. Even though it places its faith in renewed community it fails to see that socialist mega institutions are just as destructive as capitalist ones.

If we accept the importance of mediating institutions, there are two areas of concern. The first is that of public policy. For now, I merely will cite my agreement with Peter Berger's two points: "One: Public policy should protect and foster mediating structures. Two: Wherever possible, public policy should utilize the mediating structures as its agents."[70]

Second, and more importantly, ways must be found to revitalize mediating institutions from the bottom up. Drawing on my experience, I will focus on the family as a key mediating institution.

The American family has been in crisis for many years; first came the family breakdown with rising divorce rates and now the trend is the actual decline of family formation. In 1960, 82 percent of those between 25 and 34 were married; in 2000, 55 percent were; and in 2013 less than 50 percent were, and the downward trend shows no sign of ending. Marriage may have become less popular because of what Senator Elizabeth Warren calls the "two-income trap."[71] Lagging wages during the past 20 years plus the inflation of key purchases of families—houses, education, health care—have driven both parents into the workforce to try and make ends meet. However, for the less well off the cost of childcare comes close to canceling out the increased income. And the flexibility of the family unit is dramatically reduced. If a child gets sick a parent has to take off work and the family loses income. If one of the parents get sick the family income is reduced and there is no one to care for them.

The response to Warren's theory is that this is what women want. They want to be free to choose to be in the work force and not have to stay at home to raise children. However, there is substantial evidence from the American Community Survey data by the Institute for Family Studies that only 17 percent of mothers with children three years or younger say they prefer to work full time. The other 83 percent feel they have to work full time either because their income is needed or by more affluent women because they fear their careers will be side-tracked.

The serious problem of childcare has led to proposals to provide subsidies to less affluent families. If we are willing to pay for childcare for working families at, say, $400 a week, why not pay one of the parents that same $400 to stay home and take care of their own children? Rebuilding family structures may be the most important and most difficult task in making the family a functioning mediating institution in the United States today.

Thus, the modern United States economy with its high level of occupational and geographic mobility, its sharp division of work life from home life, and its transfer of education, welfare, and old age security functions to mega institutions has transformed the nature of the family. The "two-income trap" has weakened the family's ability to reach beyond itself. As a result, individual families have difficulty coping with the dichotomization of modern life.

In a new book,[72] Nobel Prize winner, economist Angus Deaton, and colleague Anne Case, provide a groundbreaking account of how today's America has become a land of broken families and few prospects for the working class and the poor more generally. They argue that this crisis is caused by the disfunctions of our current form of capitalism—the growing power of corporations, the decline of labor unions, and the adoption of misguided economic policies that have hollowed out the manufacturing heart of the economy.

Can families be a powerful force for Christian stewardship and help to restore both physical and spiritual health of local communities? Yes, but they need help. Somehow individual families must band together in groups that can provide their members with an understanding of the social world, a mechanism for acting as Christians, and a faith that will permeate the other institutions of society. And, of course, national policies are essential to reform the way present day capitalism works to benefit the already well off at the expense of the less fortunate.

It is worthwhile quoting from Pope John Paul II's encyclical, *Familiaris Consortio*:

> ...society should never fail in its fundamental task of respecting and fostering the family. The family and society have complementary functions in defending and fostering the good of each and every human being. But society more specifically the state must recognize that "the family is a society in its own original right," and so society is under a grave obligation in its relations with the family to adhere to the principle of subsidiarity.[73]

In Latin America the Comunidades de Base[74] are functioning as mediating institutions for individuals and families. In Sri Lanka the Sarvodaya Shramadana movement is based on groups of families at the village level. Both the United States and Europe lack equivalent movements. The closest type of institution has been those built on Catholic action and Young Christian Students, Young Christian Workers, and Christian Family Movement. All three are past their peak but the basic philosophy has potential for revitalization in new structures. This is what the Sarvodaya Shramadana movement did with Buddhist values in Sri Lanka.

The Second Vatican Council sets out a social role for the Christian family which is extremely demanding. In addition to the raising of children as Christian it calls for: "the adoption of abandoned infants, hospitality to strangers, assistance in the operation of schools, advise and help for adolescents, help to engaged couples, catechetical work, support of married couples and families in material or moral crises, help for the aged..."[75] And that is not all: "It is of the highest importance that families should devote themselves directly and by common agreement to transforming the very structure of society."[76] However, the bishops might have been less ambitious if they had families to raise.

Pope John Paul II reaffirms and extends the role of the family in *Familiaris Consortio*:

> Families..., either singly or in association, can and should devote themselves to manifold social service activities, especially in favor of the poor or at any rate for the benefit of all peoples and situations that cannot be reached by the public authorities' welfare organization.
>
> The social role of families is called upon to find expression also in the form of political intervention... The Christian family is...called upon to offer everyone a witness of generous and disinterested dedication to social matters through a "preferential option"  for the poor and disadvantaged.[77]

Christian families can provide real, loving care for the oppressed and afflicted while working to change the structures of oppression and affliction. Rosemary Haughton sums up the importance of families.:

> In this time of upheaval when so many innocent people are being hurt, there is an almost prophetic quality about that passage from the Council's document which firmly, almost ruthlessly, sets the Christian family at the heart of the church's mission of compassion for the world which God loves so much. That, then, is the vocation of the family in the Church to discover its identity, to fulfill its needs, to grow in unity and loyalty by responding each in its own way to the Christian vocation of loving service. In each age, the

church has called on special kinds of people to carry out its work. There is always a need for the religious congregation and other dedicated single people who can devote their lives to work beyond the scope and skill of an ordinary family. But it does seem that the church has a need at this particular historical moment for what a family can best provide: the sense of intimacy, the personal touch, a human environment of ordinary warmth and friendliness and lovingness. Very many people have pointed to the impersonality of the big cities, the big organizations, and to the loneliness and despair of those who feel rejected and depersonalized in their misery. Families, just because they have a continuous, ordinary, everyday life of their own and don't exist just to provide help, can give the sense of belonging, a feeling of positive, future facing live.[78]

Being a parent has always been difficult but in today's world it is even more so. Being a parent in a Christian family is no less so. Society awards prizes, degrees, and income to educators, physicians, and priests; not to parents. What parents get, sometimes, is "Mom, Dad, I love you," or "I don't know how you ever did it."[79] The pain, sorrow, and work that goes into raising a family and that is rewarded with "I love you" is the heart of Christian stewardship. Compassion and sharing are the products of the process. We teach our children through precept and example. In turn they teach us to be more tolerant and compassionate.

One of the primary functions of the family then is to educate its members by precept and example to see their duties and responsibilities as Christians. As the Second Vatican Council stated: "In the family, parents have the task of training their children from childhood to recognize God's love for all men. Especially by example they should teach them little by little to show concern for the material and spiritual needs of their neighbor. The whole of family life, then, would become a sort of apprenticeship for the apostolate."[81]

This process of formation is not a one way street. Parents learn from their children and from the very process of family life. What do they learn? "First of all, forgiveness." Children do not necessarily accept the beliefs of their parents. "Parents can't dismiss what has happened by blaming it entirely on others. Parents find that they made mistakes." Thus, they need to forgive and to be forgiven. Second, "compassion [which] signifies a special kind of growth and learning that reaches beyond one's own family. It is part of the necessary exchange to make humanity whole. I see only two ways to compassion. The natural way is through family life, through the vulnerability of loving, through the kind of commitment of loved ones that ends in suffering with others their miseries and griefs...In our confused and convoluted, twisted and fragmented world, we are confronted daily with those who are in need of our compassion. It is necessary only to be aware and capable of compassion."[81]

This is not meant to be a catalog of ways to educate children for Christian stewardship. Many things can and should be done. The inward focus on education naturally leads to an outward role for the family. This outward focus takes several forms. First, teaching children by example requires that the family reach outside of itself. Second, when and if the children become filled with an understanding of stewardship, they will take on as part of their life's work the alleviation of suffering.

As should be clear the family must be seen as more than an end in itself. It must be seen also as a path leading into the larger world of society. As Christians we are called to go out from the family as individuals and by way of united effort with others. Let me return to our family practices as small examples.

For years our family practiced "Kris Kringles." We drew names and, in secret, each of us did nice things for the one whose name we drew. For example, we left a piece of candy under their pillow, complimented someone, etc. It was particularly nice when someone drew a name of a rival sibling. It is difficult to give to someone we don't like, even when we love them.

Also, during Christmas before opening our gifts, Mary Ellen or I would say a prayer about the true meaning of Christmas and how commercialized it had become. One of the youngest children would them place the baby Jesus on the straw in the manger.

During Advent and Lent we begin the nightly meal with a short reading usually applying Christian love to the issues of the day racism, sexism, poverty, hunger, etc. For example, one day's reading was Isaiah 58: 6-9:

> *Is this not, rather, the fast that I choose:*
> *releasing those bound unjustly,*
> *untying the thongs of the yoke;*
> *Setting free the oppressed,*
> *breaking off every yoke?*
> *Is it not sharing your bread with the hungry,*
> *bringing the afflicted and the homeless into your house;*
> *Clothing the naked when you see them,*
> *and not turning your back on your own flesh?*
> *Then your light shall break forth like the dawn,*
> *and your wound shall quickly be healed;*
> *Your vindication shall go before you,*
> *and the glory of the LORD shall be your rear guard.*
> *Then you shall call, and the LORD will answer,*
> *you shall cry for help, and he will say: "Here I am!"*

Also, during Lent, we sometimes had a "hunger meal" (rice and tea) once a week and donated the money saved to some organization working for justice. In addition, the hungry feeling experienced gave us a small opportunity to empathize with the truly hungry of the world. However, unbeknown to us, the older children occasionally slipped out for hamburgers.

Occasionally dinner was a time when the children aired

their gripes about one another. When it got too bad, Mary Ellen would yell "Quiet! I want one positive statement about the person sitting on either side of you." One smart aleck would say "I can't think of anything nice to say about him!" "Then you may get down from the table" was our reply.

Parents are the primary educators of their children and they teach mostly by example. We have taken that seriously. Years ago, in Riverdale we were deeply involved with The Catholic Interracial Council. This led to frequent dinner conversations about the unchristian nature of racism and the demand of justice that we treat all people as brothers and sisters. This talk was reinforced by meetings, socials, and picnics where black and white families played, prayed, and ate together.

We belonged to the Christian Family Movement (CFM) in Beaverton, Ponce, and Washington and later, South Bend. We discussed the meetings at home with the children, seeking their input to the "observe, judge, act" section. Many of these meetings involved applying Christian principles to issues of the day. Over the years we opened our house to antiwar marchers, foster children, teenagers with problems and the like. The children responded generously by giving up their rooms, sleeping on the floor, and generally sharing and caring for whomever came to stay in our home, whether for one week or two years.

In 1970, Susie, a niece of Mary Ellen spent the summer with us. We got a call from the parish asking if we would take Mary Jane, a 15-year-old girl, who was having problems at home. The children immediately made her feel a part of the family, sharing and fighting with her as a sister. Teresa, Susie and she became buddies.

During the antiwar demonstrations in Washington during the late 1960s and the early 1970s many marchers stayed at our home. We and the children discussed politics and the importance of human values with them. It was a joy (but also wearying sometimes) to see the children respond with Christ like love on their own.

We used to end grace with "May the Lord provide for the needs of others." The children pointed out that instead we should pray, "May the Lord help us to provide for the needs of others." Which is another way of saying "Love your neighbor as yourself."

When Kenny was a student at Deal Junior High School, he brought home a friend to live with us who promptly stole our car and ran away. Oh well, can't have successes every time.

These actions continued throughout our time on 30th street and on into the years in South Bend. We hadn't been in South Bend long (1977) when our daughter Alice had a friend whose parents divorced and both remarried. She was not welcome at either home. Alice brought her home for the weekend and she stayed until graduation from high school four months later.

The children did volunteer work in hospitals, nursing homes, schools, etc. Matthew helped plant and care for a garden, picked the produce, and gave the food to the local justice and peace center for distribution to the poor. Alice spent a year working in South Carolina on a project for Southerners for Economic Justice. She helped organize in J.P. Stevens textile mills and worked with the local black community to help improve their conditions. The family helped support her financially, emotionally, and with our prayers. She later went to New Orleans to be a community organizer.

The time in Washington wasn't all spent on social justice projects, not by a long shot. These were the years that our oldest children became *teenagers* with all the joy and heartache that comes with that stage of life. During 1969-71 Kenny, Teresa and Matt went to Deal Junior High School at various times. These were the years that the courts mandated busing to integrate the Washington public schools. This meant students from other schools would be bused to Deal and Wilson High School in the upper northwest because these were almost all white schools and under enrolled. Unfortunately, the school district did almost everything wrong. First, they chose to bus from Anacostia which was the poorest and furthest away. Second, they added no new teachers or counselors. The result was chaos. This was also the height of the anti-war movement and the sixties drug scene.

Kenny continually had his lunch money stolen. Teresa was cornered and "felt-up" in the hallways. Classes had students with second to twelfth grade reading level. Our rather naive suggestion was to "make friends." One of those friends stole our car. They all decided to simply skip school and do other things such as spend the day at the Smithsonian. It took the school over three months to let us know that they had been absent. However, this didn't hinder their ability to pass all their courses.

In 1970 we changed schools for Kenny to Edmund Burke, a newly opened private high school. In 1972 Teresa went to Oak Hill Academy in Mouth-of-Wilson, Virginia, and Matt went to The Field School. The following year Teresa went to The Field School as did Alice. In 1974 she went to Academy of the Holy Names in Silver Spring. For three long years Mary Ellen worked at The Field School as the director's administrative assistant and bookkeeper to pay the tuition. She then came home to keep house and make dinners. She was exhausted all the time. In addition to all this, she managed to take a year plus worth of college courses at American University. As a slight help I became her substitute as lunch mother at Blessed Sacrament School.

The bad experience with race relations at Deal was offset by the close friendship we had with the Wallace family that lived across the street from us. They were the only African Americans on the block. Alice was best of friends with their daughter Quay and Mary with Russie.

Some new structures are needed to support the family as a mediating institution. One thought is to revitalize the Catholic action groups such as the Christian Family Movement that my wife and I were formed by. They were built upon the very traditional Catholic methodology—the observe-judge-act approach—first developed by Cardinal Joseph Cardijn, when he was a parish priest in Belgium before World War II.

In addition, by incorporating some of the aspects of the Comunidades de Base,[82] family based Catholic action groups can be strengthened. These communities are the basic unity of the Church where deeper prayer and shared values are lived, where personal and group objectives merge to question, discuss and act, and where ordinary people are given a sense of being the Church as a leaven in society and the world. Members of these small groups of Christians have a sense of responsibility for themselves as they celebrate the faith together. They form the Church as God's People rather than God's building.

Individual families need help in fulfilling their role as training grounds for the Christian apostolate. Parishes, groups of families, etc. must function as a network of mediating institutions. If this help is not forthcoming family life will turn inward to escape the helplessness generated by the mega institutions.

To conclude, my argument is that the growth of mega institutions, both corporate and governmental, has undermined society's mediating institutions; the family has also been undermined by economic conditions. It is the mediating institutions which always have given meaning to people's lives and through which, in turn, they have impressed their values on society. We must find ways to revitalize the mediating institutions, particularly the family, if we are to successfully cope with the problems facing us now and in the future.

The late 1960s were a time of upheaval on college campuses across the country. It was certainly true at The American University. I was department chairman at American University 1969-71, during the height of the ant-war demonstrations. The president of the university called on me several times to help calm down our students who were demonstrating on Ward Circle at the edge of campus. This disrupted the flow of traffic so Civil Defense Units were sent to break up the demonstrations. Some kids inevitably ended up throwing rocks and the police responded with tear gas. I got caught in it several times. This was also the time when drug use was rampant on campuses. I was fortunate that my dear friend and colleague, Jim Weaver,[83] could deal both with the student activists and with the administration of the university. We spent many an hour debating how best to deal with the constant emergencies that erupted. Despite being an economist, Jim had a thoughtful, spiritual side that allowed him to be calm inside himself and deal with problems wisely. His advice certainly made my life easier.

This was also a time of upheaval in the Catholic Church. The Second Vatican Council (1963-65) and Pope Paul VI's encyclical, Humane Vitae (1968) generated both positive and negative reactions. Many of the priests disciplined by Cardinal O'Boyle for dissenting from *Humane Vitae* were friends of ours. On the positive side I met two men who later at Notre Dame became dear friends—Denis Goulet[84] and Don Mc-Neil, C.S.C. Don[85] came to D.C. to see Denis, who worked at the Overseas Development Center, about a plan he had to create an undergraduate college at Notre Dame dedicated to Global Justice. When he heard that I had been hired to be the new chair of economics, he asked me to join the meeting. It was an exciting vision that eventually got translated into the more modest Center for Social Concerns. More on this in the next chapter.

# CHAPTER VIII

## University of Notre Dame

*On the Road to Emmaus*
*When you break it down*
*And map it out*
*Life is a journey*
*To the heart of God.*
*He who knows this*
*Gets there faster*
*On the straightway.*

—JEROME L. MCELROY

COMING TO NOTRE DAME in 1975 was like coming home. I entered the church while a student at the University of Portland, another school ran by the Congregation of Holy Cross. One of the Holy Cross priest faculty members in economics here had taught me at Portland 20 years earlier. Crucifixes in every classroom and a chapel in every dorm brought back many memories.

Ever since my life has been rooted at the University of Notre Dame. First, this is where our children grew up and left home. This is where our faith life has been enriched by friends and by priests of the Congregation of Holy Cross. Second, this is where I poured my heart and soul into creating a different type of economics department, with both successes and failures. Third, this is where I became involved in the writing of the United States Bishops' pastoral letter, Economic *Justice for All*. Finally, this is where we became deeply involved in establishing and operating the Holy Family Catholic Worker House. Let me take up one at a time.

## Moving to Notre Dame

In the Fall of 1974, I was asked to apply for the position of Chair of the Economics Department at the University of Notre Dame. Despite the wonderful neighborhood, I was more than ready to leave Washington, D.C. The stresses of a large city with its heavy traffic and high prices were wearing on me. Mary Ellen was under constant pressure from her job at the Field School on top of running a household of nine people. The challenge of leading the construction of an economics program built upon Catholic social thought was extremely attractive. When offered the job I said yes but only if they wanted a department imbued with Catholic social thought. If they wanted another mainstream department, I wasn't interested. The then Dean of Arts and Letters, Fred Crossen, was in complete agreement as was the Provost, Fr. Jim Burtchaell, C.S.C., and Fr. Ted Hesburgh, C.S.C.

Finding a place to live turned out to be an adventure. We rented a house near the university from a friend of the owner who was on leave in Germany. Shortly (3-4 weeks) before we were ready to move, we got a phone call telling us that the owner rented to somebody in Germany who was coming to Notre Dame for the year. The owner's friend was very apologetic. So, we had no place to live. We called the real estate agent in South Bend and said find us a four-bedroom house to rent. She came back with the news that there are none. Then we said rent two side by side apartments. Again, she came back with the answer that none are available. Finally, we said buy us a house so she and a friend, Maureen Skurski, who we had met there while interviewing for the job, bought us a large house for the price of a garage in D.C. We moved in and lived there one year while we searched for a permanent home.

Let me quote from our 1976 Christmas letter: "This past summer (1976) we moved to our permanent address. The house is large and lovely but the best thing about it is a gorgeous acre of land with lots of trees, shrubs, plants and flowers. Mary Ellen says she won't move until the yard gets too much for her to handle." It is January 2021, 44 years later, and we are still living here with no move planned. She has gotten help with the yard, however.

The move to South Bend was the 14th since we were married and when I suggested moving Mary Ellen said: "You better be sure! I will move one more time and that is it. It is not fair to the children or to me." Well, during that first year (1975-76) the university sent a notice that faculty members could buy grave plots at Cedar Grove Cemetery on Notre Dame Avenue, just as you come into the university. So, I bought two and gave her the certificates as a surprise saying, "with these I pledge to never move you again." In 1980 we celebrated our 25th wedding anniversary with a Mass at the Lady Chapel in Sacred Heart Church on campus. Our pledge to each other at the Renewal of Our Covenant was:

Wherever you die I shall die
And there shall I be buried beside you.
We will be together forever
And our love will be the gift of our life.

Since then we have celebrated our 40th, 50th and 60th wedding anniversaries. The 40+ years we have lived in South Bend have been full of good times with a sprinkling of sad times. This chapter would become way too long if I tried to relate them all or even most of them. Instead I will mention only the most memorable. Most importantly our children grew up, moved out, and began their own journeys. My work at Notre Dame, first in the economics department and then with the Peace Institute, including stints abroad in London and Perth, Australia have been important in our lives. Our faith lives have been concentrated around small Christian communities—the Catholic Worker movement, the Marianist prayer group, Shekan, and most recently a Commonweal Local Community.

As I just mentioned, our children grew up, left home, and began their own lives. I am pleased to say that each one, in their own way, has carried on the family tradition of reaching out to others, some in their career choices, others in their family and faith lives. I want to elaborate on one of our children's life, both because he brought much joy and it ended in such sadness.

Our oldest, Kenny, did not move to South Bend with us but first went into the Army, then came to South Bend, got married and had four wonderful children. He went to Baltimore as a policeman for a few years, then returned to South Bend and finished his B.A. at IUSB. He went on and got his law degree at Valparaiso Law School and practiced law locally for a number of years.

Unfortunately, he suffered from the disease of alcoholism that he could not conquer and on August 15, 2000 he committed suicide. At his funeral Mass we said of him:

Kenny was a good man. He was kind and generous. He loved his children with a deep and abiding love. He was a good son. We were, we are, proud of him.

He was faced with a terrible, ravaging sickness that sapped his strength and his spirit. He fought the good fight, but he lost. He has been born anew in a better place—one where we all will be re-united, each in our own time. He is at peace at last. It is we, the living, who must deal with his tragic death. Let us remember him in his best times:

1. We remember a Christmas when he was 3 years old. To teach him the true meaning of Christmas we suggested he give one of his new toys to a local agency that put-on Christmas parties for poor children. Kenny chose his biggest and shiniest —a wonderful fire engine from his grandmother.

2. We remember in Puerto Rico, at 4 years old, he followed a parade all the way downtown. His response to our "Why?" was: "What's wrong Mom, I was just following the parade. "

3. We remember his bright orange sport coat that his mother made for him when he was 12, for school at St. Anselm's.

4. We remember the Baltimore policeman who found shelter for street people during the bitter cold winters.

5. We remember the defense attorney who took cases with little prospect of ever getting paid.

6. We remember the laugh, the jokes, the competitiveness, the love of life.

7. We remember him at his children's ball games cheering them on, win or lose.

8. We remember our talks, sometimes fun, sometimes serious, but always loving.

And we remember too, a quote from Francois Mauriac, "Death is the last of God's mercies."

We moved to South Bend so I could take the position as chair of the economics department at Notre Dame. I did three terms from 1975 to 1984. I continued to teach in the department and also became a Fellow of the Joan B. Kroc Institute for International Peace Studies. I became an Emeritus Professor in 1999. But six months later the university asked me to become the acting director of the Peace Institute. This I did until the new director, Scott Appleby, was appointed in August 2000. He then asked me to be graduate director for the 2000-1 academic year and budget director for the next two years. I continued to teach one credit colloquia for the Peace Institute and the Program in Catholic Tradition until 2012. Retirement has been a fertile time for my research agenda. Without classes and meetings, I have been able to do much more writing.

This is a good point in the story to mention an important

"witness"in my life—Jim Langford who as the director of the University of Notre Dame Press, published two of my books and as the founder of *There are Children Here,* inspired me to seek hands on volunteering.[86]

Retirement opened up time for more volunteer work. From 1999 to 2006 Mary Ellen and I both volunteered at the front desk of the South Bend Homeless Center. That was brought short by my heart problems requiring surgery in May of 2006. Since then we have volunteered on a more limited basis at Our Lady of the Road Cafe and Drop-in Center and the attached Monroe Park Grocery Co-op; Meals on Wheels; and Michiana 5 for the Homeless.

## Economics at Notre Dame

I tried to build a different type of economics program at Notre Dame but ultimately it was unsuccessful. I was hired to build a department that used CST as the base from which to fashion a unique program. I was willing to do so because it was agreed that we would build on the unique strengths of Notre Dame as a Catholic university. The graduate PhD program was restructured to create a distinctive program marked by its focus on socioeconomic issues such as economic development, its openness to alternative methodologies such as political economy, its concern for social justice, and its reaffirmation of standard economic theory and quantitative methods. By redirecting its energies the program not only reflected the goals and objectives of the economics profession but also those of the University of Notre Dame, as specified by Father Ted Hesburgh, C.S.C., president of the university: "Notre Dame as a Catholic university, must be all of this and something more... its concern touches the moral as well as the intellectual dimensions of all the questions it asks itself and its students."

CST sees economic issues also as moral issues. Since we

are made in the image and likeness of God, concern for human dignity in social solidarity is at the core of Christian faith. Economic institutions and policies have a major impact on human dignity and thus are not only technical issues but moral concerns as well. Therefore, every perspective on economic life that is human, moral and Christian must be shaped by three questions: What does the economy do for people? What does it do to people? And how do people participate in it? Further, in pursuing the common good, we must pay special attention to the economy's impact on the poor and powerless because they are particularly vulnerable and needy.

We reorganized the graduate program to focus on three areas: economic development in the Third World, labor economics and industrial relations, and public policy in the U.S. with emphasis on income maintenance programs. This specialization reflected the type of issues central to Catholic social thought.

Let me read from the graduate brochure we published:

> The graduate program of the Department of Economics was reconstructed to create a distinctive program that is marked by its focus on socioeconomic issues such as economic development, its openness to alternative methodologies such as political economy, its concern for social justice, and its reaffirmation of standard economic theory and quantitative methods. By redirecting its energies, the Economics Department not only reflects goals and objectives of the discipline but also those of the College of Arts and Letters and the University of Notre Dame. Additionally, there is a practical reason for this reorientation. The department will never have the resources to compete with other major universities in every field of economics. By concentrating its resources, the department is establishing the uniqueness of its program and is maximizing its comparative advantage.
>
> The ultimate goal of the Department of Economics is to produce students who will have the expertise to assist in the solution of the social problems facing humanity and who will have obtained an

appreciation and understanding of these problems in the context of alternative theories of justice.

Thus, graduates in economics from the University of Notre Dame will be distinctive for their combination of technical competence, familiarity with alternative economic theories and methodologies, and their vision of social justice.

We received encouragement from Fr Hesburgh, the provost, and the Dean. However, there were difficulties, particularly in recruiting. First, economics was becoming ever more concerned with theoretical and mathematical rigor with the result that fewer new-PhDs were interested in the social economics that we were pursuing. Second, there were few Catholics getting PhDs in economics from the more prestigious graduate schools that were interested in using CST in their professional work. And, of course, South Bend, an old factory town, could not compete with the bright lights of Boston, Chicago and Berkeley. But progress was made and people in the university talked about a "sea change" in the department.

During the summer of 1981, after my second three-year term as chairman, the dean agreed to give me the funds to work on a book that I had started with my colleague Ken Jameson. In return I agreed to serve for one more term as chair. I used the funds to rent a small house in New Buffalo on Lake Michigan. This allowed me to finish a first draft of what was eventually published as *An Inquiry into the Poverty of Economics.*[87.] The book presented the kind of economics that we were trying to build at Notre Dame.

Changes at the university, particularly the attempt to emulate Princeton, engendered loud and acrimonious debate over the Catholic character of Notre Dame. Was it being undermined by the changes? What is the Catholic character? At a campus conference on the subject, I spoke on its importance for the university and for the department. I opened my talk with a quote from *The Academic Revolution*: "The important question...is not whether a few Catholic universities prove capable of competing with Harvard and Berkeley on the latter's terms, but whether Catholicism can provide an ideology or personnel for developing alternatives to the Harvard-Berkeley model of excellence."[88] I went on to say:

> "Let me make my starting point clear. I don't believe the world needs another Duke or Northwestern. It does need a Notre Dame that is truly great in its own way. It is its Catholic character that makes Notre Dame unique. The "great quest" is to build a Catholic university—for which there are no blueprints. To simply copy the great secular universities is to abandon the quest."

However, doing economics differently was not prized by the profession and low department rankings according to the disciplines criteria eventually led the university to abandon the experiment and pursue the traditional academic route with the result that standard criteria taken over from the secular academic world came to be the only criteria that mattered. In an article reviewing the later (2001-06) departmental problems, the authors said:

> As neoclassical economics achieved the status of orthodoxy and its representatives secured control of key academic journals, research grant committees, and access to prestigious academic and policy jobs, UND economists were progressively marginalized in the profession. Their professional identity, as they perceived it, was more consistent with UND's distinctive identity as an institution than with mainstream economics.[89]

As the emphasis on national rankings became greater, we begin to be questioned as to why we differed from Yale and Princeton. Why weren't we more mathematical and theoretical? Our explanations were met with ever greater resistance. Our fields were considered "soft," and unrepresentative of the top-twenty. We were publishing in the "wrong"journals. One faculty member was denied promotion to full professor—despite extensive publications, outstanding teaching, and excellent letters from people in his field—when a phone call to another university elicited a reply that he was not doing work considered central by the profession.

My successor was told by the dean to remove certain "code words"from his chairperson's recommendations for faculty members up for promotion. What were those "code words:" "social justice" and "alternatives." According to the dean, these were seen by PAC (the university wide promotions and appointments committee) as excuses for mediocrity—i.e., for not being highly ranked.

Eventually the message became even clearer—you will get new positions only if they do mathematical or theoretical economics. We finally gave-in and changed our hiring strategy to de-emphasize the fields and instead to seek the "the best person regardless of field "—where "best"was defined as technically best. The result was a department where some were demoralized, others cynical, and where the graduate program no longer had a clear focus. The consensus, among Catholics and non-Catholics alike, about our departmental mission was now shattered. The Catholic character issue was viewed with distrust at best and with indifference or contempt at worst. One faculty member was fond of giving "Catholic scholar" as an example of an oxymoron, but when challenged was only capable of mumbling some unexamined anti-Catholic prejudices. Most faculty believed that the university considered technical research as the main if not the only criterion for measuring success.

Several things came together to cause these problems. First was a naive university wide belief that preserving the Catholic character was achieved simply by hiring "check-the-box" Catholics.[90] Second was a lack of confidence in pursuing something different with the result that standard criteria taken over from the secular academic world came to be the only criteria that mattered.[91] Third was a "great man" theory which, coupled with authoritarian structures, led academic administrators to believe they understood the nature of the individual disciplines, and how they should be developed, better than the faculty in the departments. Finally, I have to admit that the department was sometimes its own worst enemy. Divisions within the department led to stalemates in hiring which convinced the administration that we did not know what we were doing.

Stories in America, even autobiographical ones, require a happy ending. Unfortunately, I do not have one to give you. We lost a unique opportunity to build a department that, shaped by Catholic social thought, could have been something special that Notre Dame gave to the world—special because it would be imbued with the Catholic character of Notre Dame.

To provide an update, in June 2019 a student emailed me the following:

> I'm a junior at Notre Dame who is looking to write a senior thesis in economics. I have been reaching out to possible advisors with the broad interest of economic justice and inequality and planning to write an empirical paper hopefully examining something from one of these topics: mass incarceration, sustainability and what motivates certain communities in the US to be more environmentally conscious, or discrimination policy and hate crime legislation. I have also been telling potential advisors that I only want to make the traditional economics honors essay "part 1" of my overall thesis, and that I would like "part 2" to be an interdisciplinary look at the shortcomings and successes of the movement for evidence-based policy within economics.
>
> My search for an advisor within the economics department has been incredibly frustrating. I have had a potential advisor tell me that "my idiosyncratic interests should not drive my thesis topic" and that I should not expect to find an advisor who would be willing to let me write on any normative topic or collaborate with a secondary advisor to make my envisioned part 2 of my thesis happen.

She asked me as an emeritus professor, to supervise her senior thesis, since she could not find one of the 40+ faculty members in the department to do so.

Let me expand my argument for what we tried to do. Economics is a lot like theology despite its claim to be a science. Traditional theology establishes first principles (which are taken as axiomatic) from revelation or natural law and then with the use of intermediate principles and judgment evaluates real world issues.

Economics uses an abstract model constructed from axiomatic assumptions about how the world works—people are motivated by self-interest, wants exceed resources, resources are mobile and fungible. Then with appropriate regard for real world deviations from the model, economists derive economic policies.

The problem, for both theologians and economists, lies in going from the general to the specific. I cannot speak for theologians, but economists are seldom trained in the specifics of how the real-world works. Rather a graduate student in economics spends all his or her time learning mathematics, statistics, and general theory. These then are used to do policy by finding a data set somewhere and applying the given tools to yield an answer. For example, the theory says that inter-personal wage differences are the result of different amounts of human capital embodied in workers. How is human capital measured? There is no thing called "human capital" out there to measure. Rather a proxy must be constructed, such as years of schooling. One result of this is that if a statistical test appears to falsify the theory, the test is rejected, and the proxy re-specified until the test comes out the way expected. That is, economists believe their theory the way theologians believe the core tenets of their faith.[92]

How do people become economists? As David Colander says in his delightful book, *The Making of an Economist, Redux*:[93]

"were an undergraduate student to ask an economist how to become an economist, he would tell her to go to graduate school. She might demur, asking, 'Wouldn't it make more sense to go to Wall Street and learn how markets work?' Getting firsthand experience may sound like a good idea to her, but most economists would briskly dismiss the suggestion. 'Well, maybe I should get a job in a real business—say, turning out automobiles.' The answer will be 'no' again: 'That's not how you learn economics.' She might try one more time. 'Well, how about if I read all the top economists of the past—John Stuart Mill, David Ricardo, Adam Smith?' Most economists would say, 'It wouldn't hurt, but it probably won't help.' Instead, he would most likely tell her, 'To become an economist who is considered an economist by other economists, you have to go to graduate school in economics.' So the reality is that, to economists, an economist is someone who has a graduate degree (doctorates strongly preferred) in economics. This means that what defines an economist is what he or she learns in graduate school."[94]

Over the past 30 years or so the graduate economics curriculum has become ever more like a program in applied mathematics with a corresponding reduction in economic history, history of economic thought, industry studies, and industrial relations. This narrowing of focus gets reinforced as the student finishes the PhD and gets a job in the academy. The greatest rewards go to those making advances in theory and publishing in the half dozen top general journals. Few articles will be accepted by these journals that do not start with the standard abstract model and then derive some new "interesting"result. Publishing in policy journals receives much less prestige and can even count against one as showing you are not a serious economist. And of course, after receiving tenure this is what one knows how to do.

Despite our failure to build a different type of department, it is encouraging that there is a growing recognition among many economists and policy makers that economies require ethical behavior in addition to self-interest. This was the heart of what we were trying to do. Let me explain why I think that Notre Dame as a Catholic University should have required at a minimum that our ethical focus be maintained and integrated with the new emphasis on neo-classical economics,

As we saw in Chapter 6, modern economics has selectively adopted Adam Smith's invisible hand metaphor, focusing on the economically wondrous effects of the butcher and baker trading out of their self-interest and ignoring his prior description of the same deistic hand's propelling the creation of a virtuous society. Virtue serves as "the fine polish to the wheels of society" while vice is "like the vile rust, which makes them jar and grate upon one another."[95] Indeed, Smith sought to distance his thesis from that of Mandeville and the implication that individual greed could be the basis for social good. Smith's understanding that virtue is a prerequisite for a desirable market society remains an important lesson. As Jerry Evensky, an economist at Syracuse, argues, for Smith "ethics is the hero—not self-interest or greed—for it is ethics that defend the social intercourse from the Hobbesian chaos"[96]

Economics and ethics are interrelated[97] because both economists (theorists and policy advisers) and economic actors (sellers, consumers, workers, investors) hold ethical values that help shape their behavior. In the first case economists must try to understand how their own values affect both economic theory and policy.

Economists, as persons, necessarily work from a viewpoint that structures the questions asked, the methods, the evidence, the answers deemed acceptable. Is this merely Joseph Schumpeter's "pre-analytic vision"or does it lead to the value permeation of theory? If there is no direct objective access to the "real"world an economist is forced to see that world through the lenses of theory. Does that mean "facts" are theory laden? And value laden? What would this mean for economic theory? The question becomes: How does one do economics in a world where facts and values cannot be conveniently disentangled?

In looking for an answer to this question, economists might need to understand, as mentioned above, that they have much to learn from Adam Smith. For example, while Smith often used the metaphor of the watch in describing how the self-interested actions of individuals worked for the good of the whole, he saw the "machine" itself as the product of a beneficent God, which moreover depended on the virtues of individual actors to operate smoothly. Smith argued that over the course of history, society advanced through successive stages, each requiring more advanced values than the previous. Smith became less sanguine about moral progress over the course of his life, but moral standards continued to play a crucial role in his work.

In the second case this means economic analysis must broaden its conception of consumer, worker, and investor behavior. All evidence indicates that economic actors (consumers, workers, firms) act out of more than calculated self-interest. Thus, the assumption of rationality may be insufficient in some cases and inappropriate in others. People's behavior is influenced by many things including ethical norms. What impact does this have upon the ability of economic theory to predict outcomes of economic actions? For example, given imperfect information purely self-interested actors might be tempted into strategic behavior that results in sub-optimal outcomes. Morally constrained behavior might reduce that opportunism.

The most fundamental postulate of neoclassical economics, rational actor theory, is that individual agents maximize some objective function. Economists and others have several reasons to be concerned with this theory. First, to the extent that economics is used as an empirical science, a faulty theory of human behavior will lead to an inability to predict and control. For example, how should government encourage people to behave in socially beneficial ways, say, to donate blood? If

people are rational maximizers, government can best achieve
its ends by providing a proper set of economic incentives for
such behavior. But if economics misconceives the way people
are motivated, incentives might fail to work. In fact, there is
some evidence that blood donations decline when a system of
cash payments is introduced. How could this be?

It is not clear how to account for the decline in contributions, but one possible answer relates to a second, generative,
role for economic theory. By this is meant its role in generating
behavior as opposed to merely predicting or controlling it.
Economics can play this role in several possible ways. First,
economics can become a sort of philosophy of life for those
who study it, leading them to behave in economically rational
ways. Second, and more appropriate for the blood-donation
case, economically rational ways of behavior can be taught
by exposure to social policies and practices that presuppose
economic rationality. Thus, even those who initially behave
according to social norms about giving blood may come to
view blood donation as just another economic transaction, once
they see people being paid for their donations. What they once
saw as a "priceless"gift they now see as just something worth,
say, $50. Thus, their non-economic motives are undercut by an
economic policy based solely on self-interest.

Ethics enters economics in a third way—since economic
policies and institutions impact people in differential ways,
questions of efficiency cannot be separated from the ethical issues involved. The question is how do you assess the differential
impact of economic institutions and policies? That is, to answer
the question of whether outcomes are desirable, ethical evaluations must be applied in addition to economic evaluations.

Let me refer again to an example from Chapter 6, about the
need for moral wisdom in economics. River blindness is a parasitic disease that has cost millions of people their eyesight and is

endemic in large parts of sub-Saharan Africa. In 1974, the Onchocerciasis Control Program, overseen by the World Health Organization, was a huge success. It prevented blindness in hundreds of thousands of people, but there was a problem: the economists involved couldn't show that the venture was worth it. A cost-benefit analysis was "inconclusive:" the people who were being helped were so poor that the benefit of saving their eyesight didn't have much monetary impact. In other words, the very thing that made the project so admirable—that it was improving the lives of the poorest people in the world—also made it, from an economic point of view, not really worth doing.[98]

A moral theory is needed to provide a framework for responding to these types of situations. For example, if one determines that value-free economics is impossible, which moral values should inform the discipline? If people do not behave simply as rational maximizers, what moral theories might guide their actions? What moral theory should be used to answer applied policy questions? All of these issues cannot be even understood, much less resolved, without some sort of a moral theory as a guide.

In addition, moral theory may be of help in answering some questions that have been only hinted at so far. First of all, in a free market society, in which firms have strong incentives to act in their own interests, is there a place for morality, or a kind of business ethics? Do firms have any obligations other than to earn money for their stockholders? During the recent coronavirus pandemic, some people and firms quickly bought up large quantities of surgical masks and gowns, disinfectant wipes, ventilators, and even toilet paper. They then turned around and re-sold them for huge markups. How should we judge this action? St. Thomas Aquinas, in the 13th century, argued that raising prices during a famine was immoral. He would have no trouble judging today's profiteers.

In our attempt to build a different economics department, we chose to use CST as the moral theory to understand economic policy proposals. I hope that a new generation of C.S.C.'s and dedicated lay faculty will rethink the mistakes of the past and start anew in building that Notre Dame of which we dream—not a clone of other universities, no matter how good, but something new, something that speaks to the world, something that we can believe in.

As a final note on my experience of trying to build an economics department at Notre Dame based on Catholic social thought, I must point out that it was a team effort and much of the early work was done by my colleagues Tom Swartz, Frank Bonello, Roger Skurski, Ken Jameson, and a number of others. The last chairman of the original department, Roger Skurski, did a spectacular job in recruiting first rate faculty who fit both the criteria of academic excellence and the policy thrust of CST. However, the die was cast; no appointments would be allowed, and the department would be split into two parts. For a short time there existed a Policy Studies Department and an Economic Theory and Econometric Department. Eventually the Policy Studies Department was dissolved and that was the end of the grand experiment.

I am consoled by a quote from Thomas Merton.

> "...Do not depend on the hope of results. You may have to face the fact that your work will be apparently worthless and even achieve no result at all, if not perhaps results opposite to what you expect. As you get used to this idea, you start more and more to concentrate not on the results, but on the value, the rightness, the truth of the work itself. You gradually struggle less and less for an idea and more and more for specific people. In the end, it is the reality of personal relationships that saves everything.

The sad case of the economics department should not detract from the reality that Notre Dame is a great university. Its undergraduate programs rival the best in the country. While its graduate programs, except for Philosophy and Theology, are over-shadowed by the best programs;[99] some of the institutes are doing world-class research. The Joan B. Kroc Institute for International Peace Studies, for example, has created a worldwide reputation for both research and training peace workers; and they did it their own way. They successfully hired talented practitioners/researchers despite lack of enthusiasm from many departments. Strong leadership by Scott Appleby over the last 20 years has been key.

## The Bishops' Pastoral Letter on the Economy

In 1980, while I was still chairman of the economics department, I was invited to be an adviser to a committee of bishops charged with writing a pastoral letter on *Capitalism and Christianity*. The final result was that in 1986 the United States bishops issued the pastoral letter, *Economic Justice for All*, that summarized the tradition of CST and applied it to the U.S. economy.[100] In my opinion, the process of writing the letter was as important as the actual message. In 1980 the bishops approved a pastoral letter on *Communism and Christianity*, written by a Yale philosopher in consultation with the bishops. They decided to do one on *Capitalism and Christianity*. A five-member committee of bishops was appointed to do so, with Archbishop Rembert Weakland, O.S.B. as chair.

The five bishops met with a group of theological and economic advisers, including myself. We quickly realized that such a pastoral would be next to impossible and be little read, the typical fate of past pastoral letters. The first questions were "which Christianity," "which capitalism?" Given the time— early 1980s—we decided to focus on Catholic Social Thought and the U.S. Economy. This was a period of recession and a time of attacks upon the poor and on poverty programs. Inflation was seen as public enemy number one and concern for unemployment was relegated to the back burner.

Hearings were held over several years with many different

groups—government officials, business CEOs, labor leaders, welfare mothers, academic economists, social action people from the church, representatives of other churches, et al. Meetings of the committee were held about once a month, usually in Washington, D.C., but also in San Francisco, New York, and at Notre Dame in Indiana.

Many meetings of the committee were held where drafts of parts of the letter were debated, amended, and tentatively approved. In 1984 a first draft was submitted to the assembled bishops for discussion. In addition, they were asked to hold consultations in their dioceses and submit back to the committee any comments and recommendations they wanted. Many dioceses held widespread meetings of the laity right down to the parish level. Also, bishops consulted with their key advisers. The bishops submitted more than 10,000 pages of material to the committee, including 500 pages written by the bishops themselves. Over the next year this material was utilized, along with additional hearings, to write a second draft of the pastoral.

This second draft was submitted to the bishops for discussion at their annual meeting in 1985. From this meeting further amendments were made to the text. The Vatican reviewed the draft and suggested a meeting with a group of Latin American bishops to discuss the section on the international economy. A meeting stretching over a weekend was held with bishops from Latin America and some of their suggestions were incorporated into the text. This third draft was submitted to the Bishops in 1986 and approved by a vote of 220 to 9. This is the document released to the public.

There are two points that need to be made clear when discussing the message of the pastoral letter. First, the bishops decided to address the pastoral to two audiences—the policy making community and to Catholics and other people of good will generally. Second, the intent of the bishops was to initiate a debate, not conclude it. That is, they wanted to show that public policy making needs to be informed by moral concerns. They hoped the letter would stimulate public discussion toward more humane policies. Also, they wanted to create church structures that would generate greater understanding of CST among the faithful. They set up an implementation office with the responsibility of getting courses on CST taught in every Catholic high school and every seminary.[101]

The Bishops' pastoral letter, *Economic Justice for All*, is fundamentally a moral document, concerned with the effects of the economy on the lives of millions of human beings. It argues that concern for human dignity in social solidarity is at the core of Christian faith. Because economic institutions and policies have a major impact on human dignity, they are not only technical but moral concerns as well. Therefore, the Bishops argue, every perspective on economic life that is human, moral and Christian must be shaped by three questions: What does the economy do for people? What does it do to people? And how do people participate in it? [para. 1] In addition, the Bishops argue that in pursuing the common good special concern must be given to the economy's impact on the poor and powerless because they are particularly vulnerable and needy. [para. 24]

Basically, the bishops have set out a moral vision to guide both policy makers and individual Christians. To quote them at some length:

> We have outlined this moral vision as a guide to all who seek to be faithful to the Gospel in their daily economic decisions and as a challenge to transform the economic arrangements that shape our lives and our world. These arrangements embody and communicate social values, and therefore have moral significance both in themselves and in their effects. Christians, like all people, must be concerned about how the concrete outcomes of their economic

activity serve human dignity; they must assess the extent to which the structures and practices of the economy support or undermine their moral vision.

Such an assessment of economic practices, structures, and outcomes leads to a variety of conclusions. Some people argue that an unfettered free-market economy, where owners, workers, and consumers pursue their enlightened self-interest, provides the greatest possible liberty, material welfare, and equity. The policy implication of this view is to intervene in the economy as little as possible because it is such a delicate mechanism that any attempt to improve it is likely to have the opposite effect. Others argue that the capitalist system is inherently inequitable and therefore contradictory to the demands of Christian morality, for it is based on acquisitiveness, competition, and self-centered individualism. They assert that capitalism is fatally flawed and must be replaced by a radically different system that abolishes private property, the profit motive, and the free market.

Catholic social teaching has traditionally rejected these ideological extremes because they are likely to produce results contrary to human dignity and economic justice.(1) Starting with the assumption that the economy has been created by human beings and can be changed by them, the Church works for improvement in a variety of economic and political contexts; but it is not the Church's role to create or promote a specific new economic system. Rather, the Church must encourage all reforms that hold out hope of transforming our economic arrangements into a fuller systemic realization of the Christian moral vision. The Church must also stand ready to challenge practices and institutions that impede or carry us farther away from realizing this vision.

In short, the Church is not bound to any particular economic, political, or social system; it has lived with many forms of economic and social organization and will continue to do so, evaluating each according to moral and ethical principles: What is the impact of the system on people? Does it support or threaten human dignity? [ para 127-130].

The bishops go on to say that: "The fundamental moral criterion for all economic decisions, policies, and institutions is this: They must be at the service of *all people, especially the poor.*" [para 24]

The following seven principles highlight the major themes from *Economic Justice for All* (and Catholic social teaching documents generally) and flesh out the call to evaluate every economic policy by what it does for people, to people and how it allows people to participate:

1. *Dignity of the Human Person*: All people are sacred, made in the image and likeness of God. People do not lose dignity because of disability, poverty, age, lack of success, or race. Ethiopians are as important to God as Americans. This emphasizes people over things, being over having.

2. *Community and the Common Good*: The human person is both sacred and social. We realize our dignity and rights in relationship with others, in community. "We are one body; when one suffers, we all suffer." We are called to respect all of God's gifts of creation, to be good stewards of the earth and each other.

3. *Rights and Responsibilities*: People have a fundamental right to life, food, shelter, health care, education and employment. If this means they must immigrate to secure these rights they are entitled to do so. All people have a right to participate in decisions that affect their lives. Corresponding to these rights are duties and responsibilities to respect the rights of others in the wider society and to work for the common good.

4. *Option for the Poor*: The moral test of a society is how it treats its most vulnerable members. The poor have the most urgent moral claim on the conscience of the nation. We are called to look at public policy decisions in terms of how they affect the poor.

5. *Dignity of Work*: People have a right to decent and productive work, fair wages, private property and economic initiative. The economy exists to serve people, not the other way around.

6. *Solidarity:* We are one human family. Our responsibilities to each other cross national, racial, economic and ideological differences. We are called to work globally for justice. In the economic arena as in other areas of life competition must be complemented with cooperation.

7. *Subsidiarity*: Catholic thought sees society as made up of a dense network of relations among individuals, families, churches, neighborhood associations, business firms, labor unions, and different levels of government. Thus, every level of society has a role to play

in ensuring basic human rights and the common good. In Catholic
Social Thought this is expressed as the "principle of subsidiarity."

In 1984, I finished my third and final term as chair
of economics. The resistance of the university's provost to our
approach to economics began to get stronger. My work with
the bishops declined after the second draft of the letter in 1985.
Thus, I had time to pursue one of my major concerns with the
economy—homelessness.

## Holy Family Catholic Worker House

Mary Ellen and I joined with three other couples in 1985
to start the Holy Family Catholic Worker House. It housed
homeless families until they could get back on their feet. It ran
for 20 years before we finally had to close and sell the house.
The stimulus for starting the house was the national crisis of
homelessness. The recession of the early 1980s combined with
the anti-welfare policies of the newly elected Reagan administration led to a dramatic increase in homeless people, particularly families. In South Bend, at that time, there were no places
for homeless families. Instead, the city gave families one-way
bus tickets to Chicago where there were beds for families.

A group of four couple including friends Ralph and Reggie
Weisser,[102] Steve and Cathy Moriarty, Michael and Margaret
Garvey[103] and us met in 1985 and discussed what could we do.
We knew our Christian faith called us to do something and
CST emphasized subsidiarity. Thus, this was our problem,
not someone else's. One of the couples had experience running a Catholic Worker House in Davenport, Iowa. Margaret
Garvey had started it and Michael Garvey worked there until
they got married, had children, and came to Notre Dame for
work. Almost like a sign, Sally Schlipmann, a worker from
the Davenport house showed up in South Bend and said she
would run one here if we got a house. So, we decided to raise

the money to buy a house near Notre Dame so we could tap into student volunteers.

Our initial fundraising drive took place around a kitchen table one winter night after a very good dinner and in the glow of much wine. We pooled our ideas and address books and began writing to like-minded and generous friends, asking their assistance in the purchase of a house about a mile south of the Notre Dame campus. Before very long, personal checks began to arrive in the mail and began to pile up in a wicker basket over which a plaster statue of St. Joseph the Worker presided. Our development program didn't really grow much more sophisticated than that over the years.

Before too long, we'd raised $19,000, but we went ahead and agreed to purchase the house for $22,000. We didn't worry too much about starting out $3000 in the hole, because we knew people would be kind, and a few of us remembered how Dorothy Day used to quote (with dubious accuracy) Pope Pius XII about how one should never hesitate "to run up bills for the poor." People were kind. Guests came, and we began to argue among each other about the quality of hospitality we could provide them. That's pretty much what went on right to the end. Our annual budget rarely exceeded $12,000, and our house was staffed entirely by unpaid volunteers who lived with the people they served.

Our small size enabled us to provide a form of hospitality more personal than what larger, and sometimes more efficient local shelters are able to offer. The precarious nature of our finances, the idiosyncrasy of our community, and the fallibility of our administration invited us to regard our guests as ambassadors of Christ. We were the first to admit that we far too often declined that invitation, but we all knew that it is a standing invitation, and we all shared a conviction that it was the central treasure of our work.

At the beginning of Advent and at the beginning of Lent we sent out a fund-raising appeal written by Michael Garvey, that usually concluded with this paragraph:

> We want to share with you the invitation which Christ has extended to us. We ask for your help in finding and greeting the Risen Christ in the suffering families who are our guests. We ask for your money, your labor, your friendship and your prayers. And we pray that the One Who rose from the dead, even as He said He would, will bless you and your family and friends.
>
> Yours in Christ the Worker.[104]

The four couples plus others over time functioned as a "board" that handled finances, repairs, insurance, taxes, public relations, etc. The director, Sally, and many successors, lived in the house keeping order and directing daily operations. The board and a growing list of volunteers helped out. The four bedrooms were continually full, with whole families in each bedroom. At one time we numbered 17 guests living there. We housed and fed people; we searched for jobs, apartments, and financial assistance ranging from food stamps to disability insurance.

In addition, we held a Mass at the house on the first and third Sundays of the month. They started at 11am and were followed by juice, coffee, rolls, and lots of talk and fun. We tried hard to bring together the guests with volunteers and supporters to form a community of support. We also held a once a month Friday night discussion (what Peter Maurin called "clarification of thought;") such topics as "Saints for Today," "Teenage Pregnancies," "Irish Music," and "Mideast Crisis." Every Thursday a potluck dinner was held at the house with volunteers and anyone interested invited to share food and companionship with each other and with the guests.

Not all things went well. There were many challenges that tested both our dedication and our good humor. One family set fire to the curtains in their bedroom and before it could be put out the fire marshal estimated it caused $23,000 in damages. Fortunately, our insurance company honored their policy despite our inadvertently not paying the premium that year. Also, fortunately, we did the repairs much cheaper because we got free labor, not only our usual volunteers but the university provided students who had to do service for misbehavior. We got mainly football players who caught the spirit of the Catholic Worker and did great work.

We also struggled with the parents of some of the families who believed that corporal punishment was the answer to any misbehavior. We insisted no hitting your kids as long as you lived with us. We lost a few families because of this.

During our last years of operation, we had ever greater difficulty finding live-in directors. Attempts to run the house with just a board that did not live with the guests simply did not work. At the time we finally decided to close the Holy Family Catholic Worker House, the proceeds from the sale were given to Michael Baxter[105] and Margie Pfeil who had recently started a new Catholic Worker called the Peter Claver House. Their focus was more traditional in that they catered to single men and women. They also established a separate Our Lady of the Road Café and Drop-in Center where homeless folks could get showers, do laundry, and get a hot breakfast. I worked the breakfast shift for the first few years and then when they set up a food co-op, I became part of that, picking up produce and buying food products for resale at the drop-in center.

The Peter Claver House has gone on to do wonderful things. They have helped revitalize the neighborhood where the men and women's houses are located. Margie and her husband bought a house there and share it with the offices of the Catholic Peace Fellowship. Catholic Worker staffers, as they have gone on to new jobs, have bought houses and are raising their families in the same block or nearby in the neighborhood. At Our Lady of the Road they have set up a shop to make coffins for the homeless. And as of 2021, Our lady of the Road, with financial assistance from the city, is providing day time shelter from the hard winter weather of South Bend.

## Faith Renewed

Needless to say, these past 45 years in the Notre Dame/South Bend area have been fulfilling and enriching for us as individuals and as a family. Someone once asked me "what do you like about South Bend?" My answer was easy, "the people." The Notre Dame/South Bend community was and is filled with wonderful people, many of extraordinary faith that shines through their actions. I have already mentioned Denis Goulet, Ralph & Reggie Weissert, Michael & Margaret Garvey, Steve & Cathy Moriarty, Don McNeil, C.S.C. and the list could have been much longer if I had the space. But I do want to mention five men who affected my life of faith, though in very different ways—Bill Toohey, C.S.C., John Gerber, C.S.C., Ted Hesburgh, C.S.C., Keith Egan, and Rashied Omar, a Muslim Iman.

Fr. Bill Toohey was head of campus ministry at the University of Notre Dame when I joined the faculty in 1975. He said the 9:30am Mass every Sunday at Sacred Heart Church on campus. Our family quickly chose to make that our weekly mass. Bill was the best homilist I have ever heard. Every sermon was at root about love. Unfortunately, Bill died in 1980 from encephalitis. He made such an impact on us and on so many others that in 2005 we held a 25th memorial service at his gravesite.[106]

My wife and I belonged to a group formed by John Gerber[108] and David Burrell, C.S.C. that met once a month for spiritual enrichment. John's reflections always hit home in their simplicity and meaning. You knew they came from his own suffering and hardship as a recovering alcoholic. As he was dying of cancer, he sent a letter to his many friends that said in part:

> I am very conscious that I am dying and that my essential inner task now is to live this death and birth with grateful and reverent attention to what God is giving me in this privileged time. By God's grace I am able to feel that this is the path I am invited to walk—that in God's mysterious and loving providence the essential tasks of my life are completed, it is not necessary for me to live any longer, and that I am being summoned toward the Presence I have yearned for since boyhood and which I have tried to serve and celebrate. I have nothing but gratitude for my life and, while I would be willing to live longer, I am at peace that God is offering me a new way.

Father Ted Hesburgh[108] was cut from another cloth. He was an administrator par excellence but a priest to his core. When the troubles in the economics department were at their height, he called and asked me to go to lunch. He wanted to know my thoughts on the situation. He agreed that the direction we tried to take of building on CST was what he wanted but now that he was no longer president, he had to stay out of it. His concern both for me as a person and for the program was heartfelt and sincere. I remember on more than one occasion him saying: "Whatever you value, be committed to it and let nothing distract you from this goal. The uncommitted life, like Plato's unexamined life, is not worth living."[109]

Keith Egan,[110] a theologian and Third Order Carmelite, has become an important influence in my life. I have benefited greatly from his wisdom, kindness, and touch of Irish humor. His emphasis on God as love has led me to rethink many things and has led me to rediscover the Little Flower's (St. Therese of Lisieux) "little way."

Rashied[111] was a student of mine in the Peace Institute's M.A. program and then a colleague there. I got to know Rashied quite well over the next few years. His family hosted one of my granddaughters at their mosque to help her fulfill a class assignment to learn about a religion other than her own. He also spent an evening talking to our prayer group about Islam and the Koran. Just a year ago he hosted several of my children and grandchildren in his home in South Africa. His faith commitment to peace and justice, his reaching out to all others, were eye-opening to one whose only knowledge of Islam came from television and newspapers since 9-11.

I have referred to them as witnesses on my journey of life. They are also companions on the Way. Our lives are intimately connected as we each try to serve God and God's people the best we know how.

## CHAPTER IX

# A Sojourner

*I have finished the race; I have kept the faith.*
—2 Timothy 4:7

IF SOMEONE IS A SOJOURNER, they have no lasting home here even though their life can be full of people, causes, and changes. My life has ranged from Oregon to Puerto Rico, through Maryland and Washington, D.C., to Notre Dame and South Bend; with stops in London and Australia; and I have had many companions on the Way. I have tried to present that journey as a kind of pilgrimage. I have sought to follow Jesus both as a person and as an economist. In this concluding chapter, I will try to sum up the lessons learned along the Way.

## My Faith Life

My faith life has been a central part of that journey. My grandparents were a mix of Baptists, Quakers and no religion. My parents did not practice but my stepfather was an off- and- on-again Seventh Day Adventist. I went to a Methodist church for a year or two so I could play on their softball team. After becoming a Catholic, I evolved from a pre-Vatican II traditionalist to a social action oriented Benedictine Oblate. Dorothy Day has been the model I have tried to emulate, all too often unsuccessfully.

Our faith has been at the center of both Mary Ellen's and my life. The call in Matthew 25 to feed the hungry, clothe the naked, visit the sick and those in prison has been a powerful force in our lives. We truly believe what Jesus said: "Amen, I say to you, whatever you did for one of these least brothers of mine, you did for me." (Matt 25:40) We have always felt that our greatest legacy is our children, that is, helping to bring into the world good, loving people who will in their turn make the world a better place. Additionally, I must not forget that I as a member of the body of Christ am the one called to feed, clothe, house, visit, and bring the Good News of Christian redemption. I can't delegate all this duty to the state. Much I must do on my own, with others in the family, in civic groups, and through the Church.

## Faith as an Economist

My journey as an economist has been both in tune with and at odds with the Roman Catholic thought in the United States that theologian Michael Baxter calls the "Catholic Americanist Tradition."[112] The central assumption of this tradition is that there exists a fundamental harmony between Catholicism (and of Christianity generally) and the United States political and economic systems. In a religiously pluralistic country, a public theology must be stripped of substantive theological content to gain currency in the nation at large. In its place is a natural law imprinted on the human mind, grasped through direct intuition combined with discursive reason.

Those traditions that separate the Gospel and the natural law dominate the academic world in which I live. The controlling assumption of scholarship in the university is that true, authentic scholarship can flourish only in an environment of "academic freedom" of intellectual inquiry from all prior assumptions about nature, the world, human society, human destiny, and especially God.[113] The result is an increasing ir-relevance of religious faith for higher education qua education.

I have spent my academic life trying to bring my Christian faith, and specifically CST, to bear on my work. But in doing so, I have had to water-down Christianity, moving from the theological to the philosophic, from Christ's love to human values. I remember a dinner party of faculty soon after be-ing hired at my first job following graduate school. A faculty member, who later became well known in the profession, asked me upon hearing I was a believing Christian, do you really believe all that s___! Later at Notre Dame several Ph D stu-dents wanted to do dissertations that openly called upon their Christian beliefs. I said no, if you want the profession to listen, your work must be cast in secular terms.

What is a committed Christian to do? One option is to keep your Christian intellectual tradition to yourself as I did in much of my work. But this carries with it a terrible disad-vantage—it reduces Christianity to an extracurricular activity. That is, it presumes that Christianity "has no real part to play when it comes to genuine, authentic, hard-core, nuts-and-bolts academic...scholarship."[114] The alternative is difficult for us secular trained academic economists to even begin to visualize and I don't have any secret answers. While accurate description of empirical reality is crucial for any economic analysis, it is equally important to locate these descriptions within a broader theological vision of the final destiny of those human beings we call producers and consumers. Here is where Christian wisdom must play a role.[115]

As I said in Chapter 6, over time I came to see myself as a social economist that questioned the free market model with its emphasis on fulfilling consumer preferences as the prima-ry criterion of human welfare and as the engine of economic growth and development. The fundamental premises of this social economics, in contrast to mainstream economics, and complementary to CST are fourfold:

First, economic actors as persons are the basic unit of the economy. Second, they act freely but within certain limits, self-interestedly but often with regard for others, and calculatedly but at times impulsively, whimsically, or altruistically, in a self-regulating economy which from time to time must be constrained deliberately in order to serve the common good and to protect the weak and the needy. Third, their economic behavior is grounded in reason and in faith, changing as economic conditions change but at times reflecting moral rules and principles, predictable and unforeseeable, and knowable with mathematical certainty and empirical precision but sometimes mysterious and beyond human understanding. Fourth, their worth at times may be construed instrumentally but finally is not reducible to economic calculus because it rests squarely on the conviction that humans have a worth and dignity beyond measure.

Further, focusing only on people's material needs misses a key point—they need their material needs met and they need love and dignity in their lives.[116] Liberals with their focus on the role of the state to help the poor and conservatives with their worship of liberty and the free market both err. While it is true that the economy is not the cause of all problems and can't solve all of them either, attention must be paid to where the economy helps or hinders people to lead a good life. Minimally this forces me to evaluate every economic policy and economic institution on how they effect "these least ones"—materially and spiritually. There is great room for debate on how best to help the poor and disadvantaged but that must always be the goal. I also realize that there are very smart and moral people who disagree with my positions.

## My Personal Faith Life

I have spent my professional life studying poverty and how to overcome it. I knew my work needed to be imbued with a deep prayer life, but action kept taking over and prayer got worked in when there was room. I developed a love for the psalms which in turn led me to the liturgy of the hours. Over the years I made half-hearted attempts to pray an abbreviated form of the Liturgy of the Hours but that usually lasted only a few months each time.

Forty-five years ago, I spent a weekend talking with Dorothy Day, my hero and exemplar.[117] If I had had ears to hear and a heart to listen back then, I would have understood her attempted synthesis between the spiritual and the material. I did not know until many years later that she was an oblate of St. Procopius Benedictine Abbey. Her insistence on the need for a structured prayer life in the midst of social action now seems obvious but it was less so then. The down to earth spirituality of the Benedictines gave Dorothy what she needed and exactly what I needed also.

I wanted and needed guidance and support. Coming across the information about Dorothy Day being a Benedictine Oblate, led me to seek more information. In her very focused biographical work, *Searching for Christ: The Spirituality of Dorothy Day*, Sr. Brigid O'Shea Merriman, O.S.F., explains:

> The esteem in which Dorothy Day held the Benedictine tradition was uneclipsed in the period following her profession as a lay Benedictine oblate. While her interest expanded, the Benedictine influence remained constant and included her fidelity to prayer, her valuing of manual labor, her concern for hospitality to the end of her days, and her unfailing desire to provide a familial community setting for both guests and staff of the Catholic Worker.[118]

At first, I became curious and then impressed. While I had made retreats at a Trappist Abbey in Oregon when I was in my early 20s, I never prayed with the monks.

Now I sought out more information on the internet since there were no Benedictine monasteries near South Bend. I found an on-line oblate class run by the Yankton Benedictine Sisters, Yankton, South Dakota. After a year of directed readings, submitting essays, and joining on-line discussions, I was prepared for my oblation. I flew out to the nearest airport, rented a car, and drove to the monastery. I received my oblation and my commitment to that community. It wasn't long before I realized that the 1000-mile distance was a major handicap. The only way I could share in the community life was to fly there. That could not happen often so I begin a search for a closer monastery where I could transfer my oblation. I discovered a fairly new monastery in Chicago, the Monastery of the Holy Cross. They accepted my transfer of oblation and that has been my Benedictine home ever since. I have been able to stay there for a few days several times a year and participate fully in the life of the monastery.[119]

When I am unable to get to Chicago, I have been blessed to be a Confrater of St. Gregory's Abbey in nearby Three Rivers, Michigan. They have a Confraternity which offers an official connection to the Abbey which is the home of a community of men living under the Rule of Saint Benedict within the Episcopal Church. They welcome Roman Catholics and all who seek to participate in the Benedictine life of worship and recollection.

While I can still be inconsistent in my prayer life, being part of the oblate community provides the sense of obligation that I need. The three promises of stability, obedience, and conversion of manners provide the anchor for oblates, crucial in maintaining one's focus amidst the cacophony of demands from the world we live in.

Stability means to not walk away from what you have

committed yourself to, for something that makes an appeal to you here and now. Stability is less about physical location than about an inner attitude. Two things were particularly important to me.

First is the realization that I am not in control, that I need to let God take control. This doesn't mean passive acceptance of whatever happens but rather as the old prayer goes: God grant me the courage to change what can be changed; the serenity to accept those I cannot change, and the wisdom to know the difference. For many years my family looked to me to solve all problems and I played right into it. When my oldest son fell victim to alcoholism, I learned from Al Anon that I was powerless. The connection to God is clear. While we must struggle against evil, we must maintain our serenity by keeping God at the center of our lives and trusting in his way.

Second is the realization that praying the liturgy of the hours is one way to keep our lives centered on God. An analogy is helpful to me. If you want to save money you need to put it first on your list of monthly expenditures not last out of whatever is left over. The same with prayer, it must be first or it will be done when nothing else is pressing. This in turn means that God moves from the center of our lives to the periphery.

**Obedience** means the art of careful listening and responding from the heart and actively. I am of two minds about this promise. On the one hand, it is clear I need to obey God's will and not my own. True freedom is found in conforming my will to God's. This is a lifelong task. How do I strip off the layers of superficial desires that pose as God's will for me? Certainly, prayer is required. Also, I need to imitate the Little Flower in treating every action, no matter how small or trivial, as acting for God. Treating each person as Christ and putting their needs before my desires is true obedience. Here is found the road to peace of soul and the road to God and everlasting life. But easier said than done.

On the other hand, I struggle with the problems associated with obeying legitimate authority. My government says it is right and good to kill people in Iraq and Afghanistan. I must say no. My bishop refuses to recognize a labor union for Catholic school employees. I must say you are wrong. My church says no to married priests. I must disagree. Most German bishops supported the Nazi war effort during World War II. They were wrong. Bishops in the southern states before and during the civil war supported slavery. They were wrong. Obedience to them is not obedience to God's will. Ultimately, we each must judge whether we are being asked to do something that is against God's will. If the action required is not inherently bad then, of course, our "abbot"—pope, bishop, priest—should always be given the benefit of the doubt but not blindly obeyed.

**Conversion of manner**s is the process of being engaged permanently and daily to improve your attitude and lifestyle. A popular book in the U.S. a few years ago talks about the purpose driven life. Benedictine spirituality leads us to change our purpose in life from the pursuit of power, pleasure and money to putting God, not self, at the center of our life and pursuits. This, of course, is also easier said than done. Everything in our culture calls us to cultivate and satisfy our selfish desires. We worship success and the power that comes with the money gained from that success. Advertising tells us we will be better parents if we just buy these toys for our children. We will be more desirable if we drive this type of car. It is our duty to buy more to keep the economy growing.

Our own inborn weaknesses respond to this conditioning and the result is a turning away from God to satisfy our selfish desires. To struggle against this requires a transformation of self that is an on-going process that never ends. And in that struggle our very weaknesses can be used with God's grace to further that transformation. Herein lies hope. My weaknesses remind me of my dependence on God. They constantly remind me of the need to be humble. And they constantly remind me of the wonder of God's mercy and forgiveness and of my need to forgive likewise. One of my favorite prayers is Psalm 51. Here is part of it that reminds me of how far I still have to go to claim I am on a pilgrimage in life and not merely a journey.

> Have mercy on me, O God,
> according to your merciful love;
> according to your great compassion,
> blot out my transgressions.
> O wash me completely from my guilt,
> and cleanse me from my sin.
>
> Create a pure heart for me, O God;
> renew a steadfast spirit within me.
> Do not cast me away from your presence;
> take not your holy spirit from me.

Let me add some more thoughts on how being an oblate has impacted my life. I wanted to know how far can people who are not monks tap into "the spiritual resources of monastic life?" Benedictine life is built upon the Rule of Benedict, written in the sixth century by St. Benedict. The first sentence of the Rule is: "Listen carefully, my child, to my instructions, and attend to them with the ear of your heart."

Listening with the heart. That is a challenge. Like many, when I pray, I talk a lot and listen little. When I try to be silent thoughts of the outside world come rushing in to fill up space. I find that if I take time to quiet down by first repeating a mantra like prayer such as "Come Lord Jesus " listening is possible even if for only a short time. I have come to realize listening requires an appreciation and cultivation of silence.

At the core of our being is an emptiness that can only be filled by God. And silence is needed to allow ourselves to open up, quiet down, shut up, and listen. It is hard to escape noise even if we want to. An example: I am in my second-floor den on Pentecost Sunday after a wonderful retreat on praying the psalms and as I write the neighbors leaf blower is making a racket. A train whistled by not long ago and cars with loud pipes go by outside too often. But the noise within me can be even louder and more distracting.

Prayer must become as natural as breathing, not forced and focused on technique. Prayer is having a relationship with God. We do so with words and in silence. What works for us now might not work in another time or for other people. We must find our way by opening ourselves up to the presence of God. We must let him in. Sometimes I must tell myself: "Be still and listen."

Praying the "liturgy of the hours ensures that God is remembered throughout the day, that time is hallowed, and that Christ's prayer is perpetuated in the world."[120] My dear friend, John Monczunski,[121] uses his own approach to praying throughout the day to create the energy to carry out his many activities. His many poem-prayers have enriched my prayer life. It is when I break up the day and the flow of time with prayer that I truly feel the presence of God in my life. God is remembered and He remembers me, our relationship flourishes. Time itself takes on the rhythm of prayer and becomes sacred. AND we are not simply praying our personal prayers but are joining the whole church in praising God and in perpetuating Christ's prayer in this world. I constantly need to keep in my mind and heart how important this is!

"Our life as Christians is not about doing anything, but about *being* something." This is at first sight a shocking statement. Jesus said the whole law is summed up in: "love the Lord your God with your whole heart and your neighbor as yourself." This is *doing*. My life has focused on doing, on serving others. But Fr. Smith goes on to argue that we will be able to do much better if we first focus on being in communion with God and we do that by prayer. This is what the Benedictine way shows us. "Each of us must reach some balance between involvement and detachment. It is good to meditate on how we can be serious about our world and still keep our focus on the eternal."[122]

Faith must not be confined to Sundays. Our faith must permeate our life in everything we do. In our work, our family life, our recreation, our relationships, in everything. This is a constant challenge. Praying the liturgy of the hours is a great reminder that each and every day is sacred. We must find ways of bringing God into everything we do. This doesn't mean we need to display our faith in WWJD bumper stickers, but minimally we must refrain from doing those things that we would be embarrassed to have Jesus see us do (because of course he does). Each day should be started with offering the day to God. I can remember when I was young and working in a steel warehouse that mentally saying the rosary while stacking steel plates was liberating and consoling. For me it is too easy to forget God as I bury myself in work or play.

God is the creator; without him nothing would be. I recognize that in the sight of God I am nothing. This is the beginning of humility. At the same time God made us little less than the angels. He loves us and I have the choice to love and serve God. At the same time that we understand our littleness we must see others as children of God that he loves as much as he loves us. I must not compare myself to others because in God's eyes we are all equal. I must focus on my relationship to God and how far I must travel to "be perfect as our heavenly father is perfect."

## Conclusion

In concluding, we would do well to heed Ken Boulding's warning of 50 years ago:

> There is a danger...in a predominantly commercial society, that people will take economic behavior as the measure of all things and will confine their relationships to those which can be conducted on the level of the commercial abstraction. To do this is to lose almost all richness or purpose in human life. He who has never loved, has never felt the call of a heroic ethic—to give and not to count the cost, to labor and not to ask for any reward-- has lived far below the peak levels of human experience. Economic man dwells in Limbo—he is not good enough for Heaven or bad enough for Hell. ...he misses the Great Virtue, and in that he is less than Man, for God has made man for himself, and he has an ineradicable hunger for the Divine, the heroic, the sanctified and uneconomic.[123]

Finally, we must remember that we are but short-term sojourners in this world. It is a temporary dwelling place, where Christians reside not as citizens with full rights but as aliens or pilgrims whose true home is in a city to come. The Church's tendency to provide religious legitimation to the debilitating and sometimes lethal workings of the market and/or the state must be resisted. What is needed is for the church—the members of Christ's body—to mount a critique of the iniquities of both the market and the state. And to carry out their obligation to love and serve God and their neighbor.

# APPENDICES:

## A Cloud of Witnesses

*To be a witness does not consist in propaganda, nor even in stirring people up,*
*but in being a living mystery.*
*It means to live in such a way that one's life would not make sense*
*if God did not exist.*

—EMMANUEL CARDINAL SUHARD

# 1. Charles P. Bailey

Pioneer Preacher

CHARLES P. BAILEY was my maternal great grandfather who died before I was born. However, his spirit dominated my early upbringing. This information is taken from Volume 1 of the *Baptist history in Oregon* and reflects how my maternal grandmother was raised and how she lived her life. She was more tolerant, but I do remember getting my hands rapped with a ruler for doing something wrong. When I stayed with her, she made sure I went to her Baptist church that still carried on the legacy of her father.

Charles P. Bailey was born in Missouri in 1850 and came with his parents to Oregon in 1852, where they settled in Douglas County. He was saved in 1873 and baptized by Elder J. C. Richardson into Oakland Baptist Church.

In 1875, after moving to Coos County, he was licensed to preach the Word by the Bethel Baptist Church, and he was ordained by the same church in 1876. Before he surrendered to preach, he fought the call for about two years, making all sorts of excuses. He was poor, in debt. and had but little knowledge of the Bible. There were no professors of religion near him but his wife and the church. That section of the country was filled with infidels and a great number of backsliders, now worse than infidel scoffers. But God's Spirit followed him, and he had no rest until he entered God's service, and by faith in god's promises he persevered.

Brother Bailey preached at Sumner to one man and his wife, the only Christians, for over a year, but at last he saw a good church and a Sunday school there. Many interesting incidents occurred in his work as a pioneer preacher.

One time a rough bully threatened to break up his meeting. Brother Bailey heard of it but never wavered. In the midst of his sermon the half-drunk bully strode in marched up to the front as if he intended to walk right over the preacher, but there was not a tremor in Brother Bailey's voice as he went on with his sermon. When within a step or two, the rowdy saw the preacher's eye and remembering his previous reputation as a boxer, hesitated, muttered something then walked out.

After laboring all week in a logging camp Brother Bailey would yet preach every Sunday. One appointment was nine miles away over a mountain that could only be crossed on foot. For more than a year he walked the nine miles and back to be at work on Monday morning. To prepare his sermons each night he would write out several passages of scripture on some topic, take them to his work, fasten them to the tree he was working on, commit them to memory and study their teachings and applications, praying for light from the Holy Spirit and he had remarkable success. (I have that book of sermons written out in his hand. They illustrate both the man and the times.)

Brother Bailey was outspoken in his views and...continued to preach over Coquille and Coos counties until 1885 when he left to take up work as a missionary for the Middle Oregon Baptist Association where he organized two churches and baptized some 40 converts within a few months' time. He continued to work in that field until 1888, when he accepted pastorate of the First Baptist Church of Dayton, Washington. While pastoring at Dayton Brother Bailey was the editor of The Baptist Sentinel, a strong Landmark paper.

In 1908 C. P. Bailey followed J. T. Moore as pastor of the First Baptist Church of Prineville, Oregon. After years of work as pastor and evangelist in eastern Oregon and Washington he passed in 1918.

## 2. Lorena Gallatin

AUNT LORENA, my father's older sister, personified kindness and a certain nuttiness. She never said a bad word about anyone and believed in the Ouija Board. I remember her séances trying to contact people dead but waiting around to speak to those who believed. Her first husband ran off and was never heard from again. She worked hard to support her family and herself. She worked in Astoria shucking oysters and spent many years in a furniture factory finishing the pieces with sanding, varnishing, etc. Her house was like a rundown antique store with her collection of dolls and whatever. I learned from her example that when times are good or difficult, you always have reasons to be thankful. Faith will see you through.

In the early years Aunt Lorena lived on a farm. I spent part of a summer with them. I don't remember much except going to the outhouse at night and waking up one morning with a cow's head sticking through the window mooing. I found the life hard, but I remember Aunt Lorena smiling and laughing.

She raised four children, mainly by herself. In the photo at the top from the left is Ena and Aunt Lorena. In the lower row is Glenn, JR, and Retha. Both Glenn and JR joined the Marine Corps at the beginning of the war and served throughout the Pacific. Glenn came home without a scratch despite being at Tarawa and a number of other island battles. JR got malaria and lots of shrapnel on Iwo Jima and other islands.

After the war Glenn married and settled on the Oregon coast farming. JR went into carpentry, got married three times, and drank too much so that he died in his early 60s. Retha never left home even after getting married and died early from cancer. Ena lived until 2009 and I saw her every summer while back in Oregon.

Aunt Lorena loved without reservation. She was poor all her life, but she radiated compassion, cheerfulness, and total forgiveness of those who hurt her.

## 3. Rev. Michael Fleming

FR. MIKE, as we called him, was a newly ordained priest; straight from Ireland, brogue and all. He was the assistant pastor at St. Cecilia's Catholic Church in Beaverton, Oregon. He organized a CFM group in the parish and functioned as its chaplain. He saw his role as a spiritual adviser only; it was up to us laity to lead. This was great training for us as we lived our lives in the secular world. It was our duty to make that world better. His guidance helped our group to be bold in utilizing the observe-judge-act process in working for migrant workers, refugees, and many other issues. He urged us to focus on our sins of omission not our sins of commission.

A few years later, during the crisis following Vatican II and the issuance of *Humanae Vitae*, he left the priesthood, got married, and worked as a social worker. He remained in good standing with the Church. He and his wife visited us in Washington, D.C. during the later 1960s. That is he on the far right in the photo, next to his wife. I am on the far left, next to Mary Ellen. In the middle is the wife of one of my old Portland friends.

# 4. Ed Smith

I MET ED and Alice Smith in 1958 in Beaverton, Oregon. They were members of the CFM group that Fr. Michael Fleming started in the parish. They were several years older than Mary Ellen and I and had recently moved from Chicago, Illinois to work for Catholic Charities in the Portland Archdiocese.

Ed was an intense, thoughtful man. He became a mentor to me. Often, we talked until the wee hours of the morning on what it means to be a Christian in this modern world. He encouraged me to follow my desire to somehow serve as a missionary in Latin America. When I got the teaching position in Puerto Rico, he organized our CFM group to support us by sending boxes of used clothing for distribution by a local order of nuns.

Ed not only talked the talk but he and his wife, Alice, walked the walk. Shortly after we left for Puerto Rico, they became full time lay missionaries right there in Beaverton, Oregon; with the support of several local CFM groups. They obtained a house for the Smiths to live rent free. A small stipend for living expenses was also provided, so they could be "full-time lay apostles."[124] This only lasted for one year as it was difficult for the Smith's to get by financially and for the CFM groups to continue raising funds.

During the year we were in Puerto Rico, Ed kept up a steady stream of letters providing spiritual advice and keeping us informed on all the doings back home. These letters are now in the University of Notre Dame archives as part of their collection on the lay apostolate.

Since I never moved back to Oregon, I lost touch with Ed. However, things did not go well for him and Alice. They got divorced and Ed eventually recognized he was an alcoholic. He did go into rehab, join AA and continued to function as a social worker at a variety of social agencies. He lost his faith in the late 1960s but in the late 1980s joined a small religious group where he became active, including becoming a priest. He remarried, had another child and became a foster parent for several handicapped children. Ed's life was marked with many highs and lows, overcoming an abusive childhood, becoming abusive himself under the influence of alcohol, but always re-covering, driven by his love of God and of suffering people.

He emailed me and wanted to restart our friendship. He died before I was able to see him on a trip back to Oregon. Rest in peace, my friend!

## 5. Joseph Powers, c.s.c.

I GOT TO KNOW FR. POWERS while a student at the University of Portland. He became a family friend and baptized our oldest daughter, Teresa. I remember one time he came for dinner and said he had been so busy all day that he never was able to pray his breviary. He asked if we could delay dinner for half an hour while he paced outside praying. I asked him about the breviary, and he explained about praying the liturgy of the hours. This ignited my lifelong interest in praying the psalms, which, in turn, led to my becoming a Benedictine Oblate.

Shortly after I came to Notre Dame in 1975, Fr. Powers retired from the University of Portland and moved to Notre Dame. He was not feeling well but he baptized our granddaughter, Heather, Teresa's first child. Thus, he baptized two generations of our family.

As he became sicker, he was moved into the medical care unit. He was then diagnosed with Amyotrophic Lateral Sclerosis (ALS), better known as Lou Gehrig's Disease. ALS is characterized by stiff muscles, muscle twitching, and gradually worsening weakness due to muscles decreasing in size. It may begin with weakness in the arms or legs, or with difficulty speaking or swallowing. About half of the people affected develop at least mild difficulties with thinking and behavior and most people experience pain. Most eventually lose the ability to walk, use their hands, speak, swallow, and breathe.

Fr. Powers slowly but steadily lost control over his muscles during the next year. Finally, he could only blink his eyes to communicate yes or no to questions. During this whole time, I never heard him complain and he remained cheerful to the end. His spirit showed through. My hope is that when my time comes, his spirit will guide my response.

## 6. Fr. Louie Putz, c.s.c.

I FIRST MET FR. PUTZ in 1959 at the CFM Conference held that year at the University of Notre Dame. After returning home I wrote him asking for advice on becoming a lay missionary in Latin America. His advice was to go back to school and get a master's degree. I took his advice, and while teaching full time at Multnomah Junior College, I went back to the University of Portland for a M.S. in Social Science with a concentration in economics.

My next encounter with Fr. Putz was after I moved to Notre Dame. With Reggie and Ralph Weissert, we organized a CFM group and Putz became our chaplain. This was pretty "heady" stuff for me. Putz and the Weisserts, original CFMers! Years before this I had read Fr. Putz's book, *The Modern Apostle* (1957), which was a major catalyst in my life as a Christian. At the beginning of the book he shows a photo of a statue of Jesus in Belgium at the end of World War II. The hands have been blown off and Putz writes, we are called to be Jesus's hands and feet in this world. That has stayed with me ever since.

Putz graduated from Notre Dame in 1932 and was sent to France to study theology. He spent his fourth year studying theology in Paris with the finest theologians and scripture scholars: Yves Congar, O.P., Henri DeLubac, S.J. and Jean Danielou; all of whom would later advise Pope John XXIII in planning the Second Vatican Council. As a deacon, young Putz worked in the Red Zone—the Communist-controlled area of Paris. He was put in charge of the parish's Young Christian Workers. At a gathering of French seminarians, he learned that the observe-judge-act principles of Canon Joseph Cardijn of Belgium were then being adapted not only by French workers but also by students, farmers and sailors. Here is where his life's work began, bringing Catholic Action to America.

Fr. Putz emphasized another principle of Canon Cardijn, like unto like. The laity should lead lay groups, students should lead Young Christian Students, workers should lead Young Christian Worker groups, couples should lead Christian Family Movement groups. He himself, after retiring from the university, established South Bend's Harvest House, a center devoted to the physical, spiritual, and cultural needs of Third Agers (as he called seniors), and the Forever Learning Institute, an inexpensive continuing-education program in which he remained active until days before his death.

Here is how his friend, colleague and brother, Rev. Theodore M. Hesburgh, C.S.C., past president of Notre Dame, summarized Louie's curriculum vitae in a foreword to the book:

> *"He lived a life filled with fresh initiatives, starting with creative work with students of Notre Dame and across North America, later with publishing ventures which announced (largely through translations) the transformations of the Second Vatican Council for an American public, then responding to the call of his Congregation of Holy Cross to implement*

*the council as rector of Moreau Seminary at Notre Dame, after which he brought the message of lay involvement in the Kingdom of God to retired folks."*[125]

To be an apostle, he once said in a homily for Pentecost Sunday, "you need not necessarily become a social worker, or a foreign missionary; you need not be a dynamic orator. You need merely be keenly alive to the needs of your neighbor, the neighbor of your immediate environment. Proximus, the Latin word for neighbor, is the man next to you. He is frequently overlooked in our ministrations of charity. ...Timely reminders, kind advice, a kind word, or sympathetic concern might save a broken spirit or otherwise lost soul. Real, effective, personal charity makes a man good, patient, not arrogant, nor repulsive. It is the master key that will open every heart. It is acquired by a constant doing of little acts of services, a readiness to serve others and sacrifice oneself."[126]

Fr. Putz practiced what he preached. And he inspired countless others, including me. His intensity could put-off some people. He told how when he came down for breakfast at Corby Hall (living quarters for Holy Cross priests on campus), some would get up and change tables. He could be fun too. At my youngest daughter's wedding reception he danced the night away with her sisters and with Reggie.

# 7. Patty Crowley

I FIRST MET PATTY CROWLEY and her husband, Pat, in 1959, while attending the CFM convention at Notre Dame. Because we had a layover in Chicago before our train left for Oregon, Patty invited us to spend the night at their house, along with scads of others. I was inspired by their work as CFM president couple over the years and by their work on the Papal Birth Control Commission set up by Pope Paul VI. In later years I got to know Patty better as she frequently visited Reggie Weissert here in South bend. Reggie would have us over for food and conversation. Patty's insight into the problems of the church and of society were stimulating and thought provoking.

She was a major force in the CFM movement that activated tens of thousands of Catholic couples in the years before the Second Vatican Council, and she was a central witness to the post-Vatican II events that triggered a crisis in the church from which it has not yet recovered. Yet Patty Crowley's deep conviction regarding what the Gospels were all about never wavered.

Patty Caron was born in 1913, the eldest of five. She was

raised in the strict, unquestioning style of Catholicism of those days. She attended Catholic schools throughout her youth, and it was while she was majoring in French and history at Trinity College in Washington, D.C. that she had her first awareness of the more challenging aspects of the faith. That awareness occurred in a class taught by Msgr. John Ryan, an early advocate of the church's social teaching. "We took the class because we heard it was easy," she said many years later. "But when he talked about justice in society and labor unions, he was fascinating. I think he opened my mind to another side of things."[127]

In 1937 she married Patrick Crowley. Between 1939 and 1947 the couple had four children plus a miscarriage and an infant who died. During this time Pat had come in contact with Fr. Putz of the University of Notre Dame who was advocating the observe-judge-act method of social change. Both Pat and Patty found the new concepts stimulating, especially the idea of applying Gospel values to family life, politics, education and social problems such as poverty and racism. The method, they believed, could be useful for married couples as well as single workers. So, they began holding couples meetings in their Wilmette home. Part of the reason the new method worked, said Patty, was because the priest-chaplain of the group was barred from commenting until the end of the meeting. "For the first time in our experience with the church, our ideas were respected," she said. "We were becoming independent, thinking for ourselves."[128]

Inspired to put into practice what they were learning, the Crowley's began taking foster children into their home. Over the years they would eventually house 14, and the last of these, Theresa, who arrived when she was three months old, they adopted. In the spirit of Benedictine hospitality that became increasingly important to them, the Crowley's also welcomed scores of foreign students and numberless visitors, so that their home was a center of constant activity. Speaking on behalf of all the Crowley children, Benedictine Sr. Patricia Crowley, Patty's eldest, said, "We are grateful to our mother for teaching us to act according to the Gospel. As we look back on our family life, we recognize that from an early age, we were introduced to our worlds diversity of cultures, races, traditions, political movements, and literary expressions. Our home was always a place of learning and of meeting people from all over the world."[129]

Meanwhile, the CFM couples concept spread to Chicago parishes and then throughout the country. In 1949 the first convention was held, and the phenomenon was formally christened the Christian Family Movement. During the next seven years CFM would reach its zenith of popularity, with some 125,000 couples participating in the United States and 26 foreign countries. The movement was training a generation of Catholics to ask questions, make judgments for themselves and take responsibility for decisions—in both the secular world and in church affairs. Fr. Andrew Greeley, a longtime friend of the Crowley's, said, "In terms of lay activism, Patty was the most important woman of her time, and CFM was the most important movement of the preconciliar church."[130]

Here is how Rose Lucey in her book, *Roots and Wings*, recalled the 1965 convention at Notre Dame University, which drew 5,000 people. "The prophets were among us: Jesuit Gustave Weigel, George Schuster, Dr. Martin Marty, John Tracy Ellis...John McKenzie, Dan Berrigan, Henri Nouwen, Gregory Baum, Tom Dooley, Bishop Charles Buswell. ... And always in the background...Pat and Patty Crowley: Patty to mother each person at the convention, keep things organized, the foil for all of Pat's jokes; and Pat, full of wisdom, pretending he was not a great thinker, both of them mentors for the thousands of couples who came. ... And with Pat and Patty, their own children and all the other children who happened to be living with them at the time."[131]

In 1964 they were invited by Pope Paul VI to take part in the Papal Birth Control Commission, originally created by Pope John XXIII to advise the papacy on the morality of new contraceptive methods. At their second meeting with the commission in 1966, the Crowley's presented the results of a sociological survey of married couples that they had authorized. It revealed how painful (and unsuccessful) most Catholic couples found the practice of rhythm, the church's sole approved method of birth control.

Patty's speech to the Birth Control Commission expressed the feelings of most in CFM, including ourselves:

*We have been blessed with only 5 children of our own but have housed more than a dozen foster children during the past 20 years under the supervision of the Catholic Charities. In addition to an active professional life as a lawyer and the duties of a housewife, together during the past 20 years we have devoted much of our spare time to organizing and activating couples in the Christian Family Movement. This experience brought us into close contact with thousands of apostolic, intelligent young families who by their lives have demonstrated a great love for the Church. ...*

*CFM is known to be a sympathetic setting for large families. Since being told of our appointment and being authorized to consult our contemporaries, we have been shocked into a realization that even the most dedicated, committed Catholic couples are deeply troubled by this problem. We have gathered hundreds of statements from many parts of the United States and Canada and have been overwhelmed by the strong consensus in favor of some change. Most expressed a hope that the positive values in love and marriage need to be stressed and that an expanded theology of marriage needs to be developed.*

*It is in fact largely our very love for children as persons and our desire for their full development as committed Christians that leads us to realize that numbers alone and the large size of a family is by no means a Christian ideal unless parents can truly be concerned about and capable of nurturing a high quality of Christian life.*[132]

The Crowley's were outspoken in their own views on the subject. During a heated discussion about how the church could save face if it were to allow couples to decide how to limit offspring, Marcelino Zalba, a Spanish Jesuit member of the commission, asked, "What then with the millions we have sent to hell" if the rules are relaxed? Patty immediately responded in what became perhaps her most memorable quote. "Fr. Zalba," she said, "do you really believe God has carried out all your orders?"[133]

In the end, the commission recommended overwhelmingly that the strict prohibition against contraception should be lifted, and a belatedly summoned "overseer" commission of cardinals and bishops concurred with the decision. "I don't think there was a doubt in any of our minds that the pope would follow the commission report," Patty said at the time. But after a two-year wait Paul VI issued the encyclical *Humanae Vitae*, which flatly rejected the commission report and declared the prohibition would remain in force.[134]

The decision came as an especially hard blow to the Crowley's. Patty and Pat were quite open and public in expressing their disappointment. Some 25 years after *Humanae Vitae* she shared her feelings in an article she wrote for NCR: "I feel betrayed by the church. The pope continually states that birth control is evil, yet I know that couples must be practicing birth control. One never hears from the pulpit that birth control is intrinsically evil and should not be practiced. Is the church hypocritical?... I long for a church that is honest about its teachings, that admits its errors and faces the effects of rigidity with openness."[135]

She remained a supporter (and sometimes critic) of CFM as it shifted its emphasis and grew smaller in the 1980s and

'90s, even as her personal efforts turned more toward direct works of social justice and charity. In 1985 she and a small group of associates founded Deborah's Place, which has become the largest private, multiservice shelter operation for homeless women in Chicago. For many years, Pat and Patty's eldest child, Sr. Patricia (Patsy) Crowley, was executive director of Deborah's Place.

As her health declined, Patty provided a blunt, typically pithy summary of the spiritual outlook that guided her life. "I say the only important thing is Jesus' message, and the rest of the rules are for the birds. So give food to the hungry, give drink to the thirsty, help the sick and visit those in prison. That's what I do."

## 8. Archbishop Edward Howard

WHEN I MET ARCHBISHOP HOWARD in 1959, he was 82 years old and had been archbishop of Portland since 1926. He retired a few years later in 1966 and died in 1983 at age of 105. My meeting with Archbishop Howard about sponsoring refugees was short but left a deep impression on me. When I told him that I sought his permission to begin speaking at parishes to encourage them to sponsor Dutch-Indonesian refugees, he stopped me and said: "Don't ask for permission, I might have to say no." He went on to say this program of sponsoring refugees is exactly what Catholic laity should be doing.

Archbishop Howard's response has stuck with me. The laity should not be seeking permission. We should be seeing action for justice as *our calling.*

I want to mention one other remembrance of Archbishop Howard. Mary Ellen and I were at a small gathering and when he entered, each person in turn genuflected and kissed his episcopal ring. When it came to Mary Ellen's turn, the archbishop, noticing she was obviously quite pregnant, kept her from kneeling and shook hands instead.

## 9. Estelle and Mario Carota

ESTELLE AND MARIO CAROTA are a remarkable couple. Mario was born in Arnold, Pennsylvania and raised in Roosevelt, New York. He studied ceramic engineering at Alfred University in New York where he took up flying. He joined the Navy during WWII and was a flight instructor and member of a special drone project for that service. He married Estelle Field on December 24, 1942 and raised a family of nineteen children, including 12 adopted that were considered "unadoptable" by the authorities.

Mario worked as a teacher, an atomic engineer at the University of California, Berkeley, Radiation Laboratory, but gave up his job when he became aware of the implications of his work. They are best known for their work as lay missionaries in the mountains near Mexico City, helping poor campesinos organize co-operatives and distributing powdered milk, corn, beans, and other food donated by Catholic friends and the government of Canada. They helped build two schools, a trade center and a hospice house.

The Carota's tell of a credit union that must be almost unique in the history of banking and is also a model of how the poorest of the poor can help themselves and each other when they have the right spirit, which is the spirit of Christ derived from a study of the Gospel. I quote:

> *"A remarkable example of the ability of the poor to use their own meager resources to be of service to their community is the zero-interest credit union in the barrio of San Martin in Malinaco. Its 20-odd members saved about US$400 over the past three years by bringing 25 to 50 cents each week to their meetings. The fund is used to make emergency loans to people in their community as well as to the members of the coop. The credit union makes these no-interest loans as a way of serving their community in the name of Christ. The miraculous part of all this, considering the incredible economic problems facing these poor people, is that all the loans*

*have been repaid without fail. The revolutionary part is that, consid-*
*ering the total impossibility of their obtaining loans from any bank, this*
*credit system is actually working to serve the poor. And in the process the*
*poor are receiving spiritual development from their weekly sharing of*
*Scripture and also great personal development from being the owners and*
*managers of their own bank.*"[136]

I met them long ago at the Crowley's house after the 1959 CFM Conference at the University of Notre Dame. The family of two parents and 19 children arrived and left in a big yellow school bus that they had outfitted as a camper. They, we, and several other families spent the night before leaving the next day for our respective homes. The Carota's were headed back to Mexico. We spent the evening until the wee hours listening to Mario talk about their adventures. It was a short time to know them, but it had a profound effect on me. If they could do what all they did with all those kids, why couldn't we?

In the years after that first meeting, we seldom were in touch, except for the CFM conference at Notre Dame in 1976 and then sometime in the 1990s they sent a homemade video of their lives together following Jesus wherever he called—California, Mexico, Canada.

In his later years Mario cared for his ailing wife, Estelle, until she died in 2004 and built over seven hundred stained glass crucifixes which he donated to all who wanted them. Mario passed away at his Hollister residence on June 17th, 2017 at the age of 96 years.

# 10. Ivan Illich

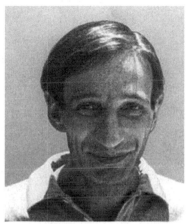

Ivan Illich, thinker, born September 4, 1926;
died December 2, 2002

AS I WROTE IN CHAPTER 4, I worked in Puerto Rico
with Msgr Ivan Illich at his Center for Intercultural Communications. This was set up in 1956 to introduce priests and
nuns, going to serve in Latin America, to Spanish and poor
folks' culture. He was a fascinating guy. He used to come
over about 11pm and stay until 2-3 am talking endlessly about
things in Puerto Rico and how to overcome poverty. He was
the vice-chancellor of the university but refused to lead the
standard lifestyle of the other priests and nuns on campus. At
one point he lived with one particular order of priests in their
house on campus but slept on the floor and ate only beans and
rice instead of their full course meals. They got so upset with
him that they forced him to leave. He then bought a one room
"house" on stilts for $35, with no running water or electricity.
He slept and said Mass there for the poor people in the neighborhood. He left Puerto Rico after the elections in November
1960 as the local bishops opposed the Popular Democratic

Party and endorsed a Christian Democratic Party; that Illich spoke out against. He went on to start the new intercultural institute in Cuernavaca, Mexico. He invited me to join him there when I finished a PhD in economics. He insisted that if I wanted to be heard I had to go back to school for the PhD. That is what made us leave after only one year.

Since it took five years to finish my PhD and we had three more children by then, it became clear that we could not afford to join Ivan in Mexico. After that, I saw him 2-3 times when he gave lectures in Washington, D.C. I did follow his work in Mexico, reading the newsletter and reports plus reading his many books. Years later, while at Notre Dame, I became friends with a retired cardiologist who did a master's degree in ethics. Turned out he was a good friend of Illich and I got occasional reports on his personal life.

Both in his person and in his writings, Ivan had a profound effect on my thinking. I particularly remember him saying, late one night in Puerto Rico, you need to love people for themselves, not just because Jesus loves them, or that is how you love Jesus. I have wrestled with his point ever since.

Ivan died of cancer at age 76. He was one of the world's great thinkers, a polymath whose output covered vast terrains. He worked in 10 languages; he was a jet-age ascetic with few possessions; he explored Asia and South America on foot; and his obligations to his many collaborators led to a constant crisscrossing of the globe in the last two decades. His critique of modernity was founded on a deep understanding of the birth of institutions in the 13th century, a critical period in church history which enlightened all of his work, whether about gender, reading or materiality. He was far more significant as an archaeologist of ideas, someone who helped us to see the present in a truer and richer perspective, than as an ideologue.

His charisma, brilliance and spirituality were clear to anyone who encountered him; these qualities sustained him in a heroic level of activity over the last 10 years in the context of terrible suffering caused by a disfiguring cancer. Following the thesis of his book, *Medical Nemesis*, he administered his own medication against the advice of doctors, who proposed a largely sedative treatment which would have rendered his work impossible.

Our many discussions that went long into the night continued to motivate me as frustration and depression threatened to make me give up on whatever battle I was engaged in at the time. They still do.

# 11. Dorothy Day

DOROTHY DAY'S personal journey included years as a re-
bellious bohemian, ultimately finding meaning in life through
the Catholic faith. At first, however, even her new religious
faith brought Dorothy no clear purpose in life. Then she met
Peter Maurin, who convinced her that radical social reform
and the Roman Catholic faith could be united. Dorothy now
found a purpose in life that would remain with her for the remainder of her days. Together with Peter she founded a movement which would carry Jesus's original message to the most
dispossessed of workers. They would prove that Catholicism
served the poor as well as the rich, the weak better than the
mighty. They established a newspaper and a house of hospitality. The paper sold for a penny a copy and still does. There are
over 200 houses of hospitality today and several newspapers.

How did Dorothy influence me? I know her mainly
through her writings; her autobiography, her letters, her
journals, writings in The Catholic Worker, and biographies

by Jim Forest, her granddaughter, Kate Hennessy, and many others, from which I have liberally borrowed; and through one weekend together in August 1961, that I wrote about in Chapter 5. She inspired me to seek to love and serve God and God's people, to be Jesus' hands and feet in this world. Even though I fail all too often, her perseverance leads me to keep trying.

First, she taught me that justice begins on our knees. She was first and foremost a praying person. I see her first of all on her knees praying before the Blessed Sacrament. I see those long lists of names she kept of people, living and dead, to pray for. I see her at Mass, I see her praying the rosary, I see her going off for Confession each Saturday evening. I see her on her knees after mass picking up the crumbs of the Eucharist that Fr. Dan Berrigan had scattered over the floor.

"We feed the hungry, yes," she said. "We try to shelter the homeless and give them clothes, but there is strong faith at work; we pray. If an outsider who comes to visit us doesn't pay attention to our praying and what that means, then he'll miss the whole point." What makes her life inspiring, what gave her direction and courage and strength to persevere, what enabled her deep attentiveness to others? It was her spiritual and sacramental life.

Second, she taught me that justice is not just a project for the government, do-good agencies, or radical movements designing a new social order in which all the world's problems will be solved. It's for you and me, here and now, right where we are.

Jesus did not say "Blessed are you who give contributions to charity" or "Blessed are you who are planning a just society." He said, "Welcome into the Kingdom prepared for you since the foundation of the world, for I was hungry, and you fed me." At the heart of what Dorothy did were the works of mercy. For her, these were not simply obligations the Lord imposed on his followers. As she said on one occasion to Robert Coles, "We are here to celebrate him through these works of mercy."

Third, she taught me that the most radical thing we can do is to try and find the face of Christ in others, and not only those we find it easy to be with but those who make us nervous, frighten us, alarm us, or even terrify us. "Those who cannot see the face of Christ in the poor," she used to say, "are atheists indeed."

Dorothy was an orthodox Catholic. This means she believed that Christ has left himself with us both in the Eucharist and in those in need. "What you did to the least person, you did to me."

And she said: "The Gospel takes away our right forever, to discriminate between the deserving and the undeserving poor."

Her searching of faces for Christ's presence extended to those who were her "enemies." They were, she always tried to remember, victims of the very structures they were in charge of.

She sometimes recalled the advice she had been given by a fellow prisoner named Mary Ann, a prostitute, when she was in jail in Chicago in the early 1920s: "You must hold up your head high and give them no clue that you're afraid of them or ready to beg them for anything, any favors whatsoever. But you must see them for what they are—never forget that they're in jail too."

Fourth, she taught me that beauty is not just for the affluent. Tom Cornell tells the story of a donor coming into the Catholic Worker and giving Dorothy a diamond ring. Dorothy thanked her for it and put it in her pocket. Later a rather demented lady came in, one of the more irritating regulars at the house. Dorothy took the diamond ring out of her pocket and gave it to the woman. Someone on the staff said to Dorothy, "Wouldn't it have been better if we took the ring to the diamond exchange, sold it, and paid that woman's rent for a year?" Dorothy replied that the woman had her dignity and could do what she liked with the ring. She could sell it for rent money or take a trip to the Bahamas. Or she could enjoy wearing a diamond ring on her hand like the woman who gave it away. "Do you suppose," Dorothy asked, "that God created diamonds only for the rich?" Dorothy's granddaughter's biography's title is *Dorothy Day: The World Will be Saved by Beauty.*

Fifth, she taught me that meekness does not mean being weak-kneed. There is a place for outrage as well as a place for very plain speech in religious life. Someone suggested Dorothy should speak in a more polite, temperate way. Dorothy replied: "I hold more temper in one minute than you will hold in your entire life."

Sixth, she taught me to focus on the "little way." The phrase was one Dorothy borrowed from Saint Therese of Lisieux, the Little Flower, of whom she wrote a wonderful book, *Therese,* about. Change starts not in the future but in the present, not in Washington or on Wall Street but right here with me.

Change begins not in the isolated dramatic gesture or the petition signed but in the ordinary actions of life, how I live minute to minute, what I do with my life, what I notice, what I respond to, the care and attention with which I listen, the way in which I respond.

As Dorothy once put it: "Paperwork, cleaning the house, dealing with the innumerable visitors who come all through the day, answering the phone, keeping patience and acting intelligently, which is to find some meaning in all that happens—these things, too, are the works of peace, and often seem like a very little way."

Or again: "What I want to bring out is how a pebble cast into a pond causes ripples that spread in all directions. Each one of our thoughts, words, and deeds is like that."

What she tried to practice was "Christ's technique," as she put it, which was not to seek out meetings with emperors and important officials but with "obscure people, a few fishermen and farm people, a few ailing and hard-pressed men and women."

Seventh, she taught me to love the church and at the same time to speak out honestly about its faults. She used to say that the net Saint Peter lowered when Christ made him a fisher of men caught "quite a few blowfish and not a few sharks."

Dorothy said many times that "the church is the cross on which Christ is crucified." When she saw the church taking the side of the rich and powerful, forgetting the weak, or saw bishops living in luxury while the poor are thrown the crumbs of "charity," she said she knew that Christ was being insulted and once again being sent to his death.

"The church doesn't only belong to the officials and bureaucrats," she said. "It belongs to all people, and especially its most humble men and women and children."

At the same time, I learned from her not to focus on the human failings so obvious in every church, but rather to pay attention to what the church sets its sights on. We're not here to pass judgment on our fellow believers, whatever their role in the church, but to live the gospel as wholeheartedly as we can and make the best use we can of the sacraments and every other resource the church offers to us.

Cardinal John O'Connor remarked from the pulpit of St. Patrick's cathedral regarding his nomination of her for sainthood:

> Dorothy Day saw the world at large turned into a huge commercial marketplace where money means more than anything else. She saw people

*turned into tools of commerce. She saw the family treated as a market-place. She reminded us frequently enough that the Church herself could become simply a marketplace. She loved the Church, and she was immensely faithful to the Church... But she recognized that we poor, weak human beings—people like you, people like me—could turn the Church into nothing but a marketplace.*

Last and most importantly, she taught me that I am here to follow Christ. Not the pope. Not the president of the United States. Not even Dorothy Day or any other saint.

Christ has told us plainly about the Last Judgment, and it has nothing to do with belonging to the right church or being theologically correct. All the church can do is try to get us on the right track and keep us there. We will be judged not on membership cards but according to our readiness to let the mercy of God pass through us to others. "Love is the measure," Dorothy said again and again, quoting Saint John of the Cross.

Hers was a day-to-day way of the cross, and just as truly the way of the open door.

"It is the living from day to day," she said, "taking no thought for the morrow, seeing Christ in all who come to us, and trying literally to follow the gospel that resulted in this work."

"The greatest challenge of the day is: how to bring about a revolution of the heart, a revolution which has to start with each one of us? When we begin to take the lowest place, to wash the feet of others, to love our brothers [and sisters] with that burning love, that passion, which led to the Cross, then we can truly say, 'Now I have begun.'"

## 12. Hans and Madeline Furth

I MET HANS AND MADELINE in 1959. He was finishing a PhD in Psychology at the University of Portland as I was finishing a M.S. in Social Science. He went to the Catholic University of America in Washington, D.C. as a faculty member. Sometime later we moved to Puerto Rico. One year later, in August 1961, I was accepted in graduate school for a PhD in economics at the University of Maryland. The Furth's had bought a house and invited us to stay with them while we searched for housing. We stayed for three weeks.

House hunting turned out to be difficult. My salary as a teaching assistant was $1800 a year. When I told prospective landlords what I earned they just laughed and said no. Hans convinced me to lie and say I made $6000, but that didn't work either. With four children, even $6000 wasn't enough. Finally, however, we found a flat in a house in Silver Spring that didn't ask how much I made and rented to us. As noted in the text I had to find an additional job, which I did at Trinity College. I must point out that this flat was hardly big enough to accommodate our large and growing family. Mary Ellen was pregnant with our fifth child, who was born in July of 1962. We found a house in Riverdale, Maryland that had lots of room and was cheap, but we had no down payment. Hans and Madeline loaned us a $1000 so we could buy the house.

The highlight of our time staying with the Furth's was when Dorothy Day spent the weekend there also, while attending a conference. We had many discussions while she held our baby, Alice, on her lap.

In August 1968 we moved from Riverdale into Washington, D.C. We soon had the opportunity to repay some of the Furth's kindness. One of their sons accidently caught their house on fire while playing with matches. Three weeks after we moved, the Furth's said they were moving in with us, all 10 of them—Hans, Madeline, Jeanie (Madeline's cousin) and seven children. They stayed for a month.

During these years we got to know the Furth's well. Some of their children and some of ours became friends. Our houses were only a few blocks apart. They had fascinating backgrounds that are worth noting. I knew Hans much better than Madeline, so I have more to say about him.

Hans Furth was born to Jewish parents in Austria and baptized into the Catholic Church at the age of 16. As a child, he was trained in classical piano and active in Austrian Boy Scouts. Shortly after the 1938 Anschluss of Austria into Germany, Furth fled the Nazis; first to Croatia, as a dependent of his mother who had married an elderly Croatian acquaintance to gain entry into that country. Upon achieving the age of majority, Hans would have been evicted from Croatia, so he obtained a visa to travel to Belgium. In route, he jumped off the train in Switzerland, and lived illegally with a Swiss family.

From Switzerland, he obtained a visa to travel to the United Kingdom by volunteering to work in the Australian outback. After arriving in England, he abandoned the Australian venture, and lived with a professor of music. He graduated from the Royal Academy of Music in London in 1940 hoping to become a concert pianist and, after being interned as an enemy alien, performed at internment camps for Jewish refugees in various locations throughout Britain, as well as Hutchinson Camp on the Isle of Man. He spent the next decade as a monk in the Carthusian order and then emigrated to North America to study with Karl Stern.

Hans received a master's degree in clinical psychology from the University of Ottawa in 1954 and a doctorate degree in psychology from the University of Portland in 1960. In the same year, he became a professor of psychology at Catholic University of America, in Washington, D.C. He specialized in learning theory and became quite well known for working with deaf children.

Madeline was the daughter of the late Daniel Steen, Norway's Ambassador to Canada from 1948 to 1951. They met in Canada and were married there.

Hans and Madeleine were active in the civil rights movement, offering their home in Washington, D.C., to protesters who marched with Martin Luther King Jr. in August 1963. They had seven children and a score of grandchildren. Madeline was very active in the League of Women Voters

In the last decade of his life, Hans often performed at area nursing homes, playing works of Bach, Beethoven, and Mozart. After retiring from full-time teaching in 1990, Hans focused on writing about his past. He completed a manuscript titled "Society Faces Extinction: The Psychology of Auschwitz and Hiroshima," which explores the idea that the capacity to commit genocide is conceivable in many cultures.

Hans and Madeline, though estranged in their later years, were devout Christians and social activists, particularly Madeline. Basically, we were companions on the Way. They not only helped us materially but the example of their life with Han's intellectual focus and Madeline's activism, was both stimulating and challenging.

# 13. Jim Weaver

Ken Jameson, Jim Weaver and Chuck Wilber

JIM WEAVER was a colleague and my best friend that I dearly loved. I first met Jim in 1963 shortly after he came to American University and I was being interviewed for a position there. I was amazed by his ability to synthesize the issues facing poor countries, the issue we both were working on. Over the next 11 years teaching together I was awed by his ability to articulate the fundamental principles of economics and to critique them at the same time. And he did so while treating each student, conservative or liberal, as a fellow human being deserving of respect. For the past 50+ years we have been colleagues and friends even though we have lived in different cities during the past 40 years. We made a habit of getting together every two or three years for a two-day brain storming session with our colleague Ken Jameson. During these sessions we devised plans to solve the world's current problems, if the powers that be would just listen. Of course, they didn't but the fellowship was wonderful. Jim loved poetry and insightful quotes. Here is one from Thomas Merton that fits Jim and our gatherings:

*Do not depend on the hope of results. You may have to face the fact that your work will be apparently worthless and even achieve no result at all, if not perhaps results opposite to what you expect. As you get used to this idea, you start more and more to concentrate not on the results, but on the value, the rightness, the truth of the work itself. You gradually struggle less and less for an idea and more and more for specific people. In the end, it is the reality of personal relationships that saves everything.*

Jim lived through many years of heart disease before getting a heart transplant and living 20 years more. After a near death episode in 1994, he wrote up his experience for a paper prepared for a Wesley Seminary class in Death, Dying and Bereavement:

*God has plans for me. I'm not sure exactly what they are, but I know they involve helping other people struggling with issues of aging, chronic illness, death, and bereavement. It is still not clear to me exactly what format my work will take, but that will come.*

*I am reminded of a hymn from the Pilgrim hymnal that we sing at Westmoreland Congregational Church.*

### COME LABOR ON
Come, labor on.
*Who dares stand idle
on the harvest plain
While all around us
waves the golden grain?
And to each servant
does the Master say,
"Go work today."*

*And now that I feel that I have dealt with death, I feel ready to deal with life. As I do, I have many of the same feelings as Ulysses in Tennyson's poem by that name. Ulysses is an old man and is the speaker.*

*Old age has yet his honor and his toil;*
*Death closes all: but something ere the end,*
*Some work of noble note, may yet be done,*
*Not unbecoming men that strove with Gods.*
*The lights begin to twinkle from the rocks:*
*The long day wanes: the slow moon climbs: the deep*
*Moans round with many voices. Come, my friends,*
*'Tis not too late to seek a newer world.*

*And it is not too late to seek a newer world. I will do battle with the disease, I will do battle with injustice, and I will try to help others dealing with illness and death. I will labor on. I will do battle. I remember Blake's words from "Jerusalem."*

*I shall not shrink from mental fight,*
*Nor shall my sword sleep in my hand*
*Till we have built Jerusalem*
*In England's green and pleasant land.*

After retiring from teaching, Jim went to Wesley Seminary and became an ordained minister in the United Church of Christ. He led a small church congregation in suburban Maryland and went all over the country officiating at baptisms and weddings. To the end he preached the need for all to emulate the Good Samaritan in our daily lives.

The last time I saw Jim was a few months before he died. He and his wife, Mary, were living in a retirement home in Washington, D.C. He had just been moved from independent living with Mary to assisted living in another part of the complex. Alzheimer's was just beginning to obscure his mental and moral vitality. Every now and then the Jim of old would emerge. I remember him saying how fortunate he was. I agree, he had good friends, a great wife, a loving God, and a life well spent. We were companions on the Way.

# 14. Denis Goulet

I KNEW AND LOVED DENIS GOULET as a colleague and as a dear friend. I first met Denis at a conference on Third World poverty in 1970 and was amazed by his ability to synthesize the issues facing poor countries. We met again in 1972 when we were on a panel together. Again, I was awed by his ability to articulate the fundamental issues. Since 1978 until his death in 2006, we were both colleagues and friends. Thus, I feel honored to say he was an important witness in my life and a vital companion on the Way. Let me reflect on his life as a development ethicist and as a man.

## Development Ethicist

Denis was a pioneer in the interdisciplinary study of development ethics, in fact he is considered by many to be its founding father. Denis came to the study and practice of development ethics in a roundabout way. Following initial university studies (1948-50) centered on business administration his major interest turned to the philosophy of religion, joined the Paulist Order, earned a B.A. in 1954 and by 1956 he had acquired a master's degree with a thesis on a critical comparison of Thomistic natural law ethics and Kierkegaard's distinctive religious existentialism.

By then he had become disenchanted with the purely academic study of philosophical and religious questions, and he searched for a way of doing philosophy and practicing religion in a hands-on fashion. The example set by the French philosopher Simone Weil (1909-1943) and the "worker priests," who shared life's hardships and economic vulnerabilities of poor workers so as to give concrete embodied expression to human solidarity, fired his imagination. Equally appealing to him, as one searching for 'what to do with his life,' was the story of Charles de Foucauld (1858-1916), French nobleman become, successively, military officer, geographical explorer, Trappist monk, and religious hermit living for years in the Sahara while refraining from proselytizing and cultural conquest simply to share the life of native Muslim populations as a sign of God's love for all human creatures. Leaving the Paulist's, Denis lived and worked (1957-58) in France, Spain, and Algeria with small fraternities inspired by de Foucauld's life and writings, as a participant observer and potential prospective candidate to this innovative Catholic religious order.

He then enrolled (1959) in the recently opened Paris-based graduate school for development planning, to begin a new education as a "philosopher of development," earning a master's degree in social planning. There Fr. Lebret (1897-1966) took Denis under his wing and served as his personal guide—in France (1959), Lebanon (1960), and Brazil (1961). He urged him, and assisted in many practical ways, to define his life's work to become a development ethicist operating in its several arenas—theory, analysis, pedagogy, planning, and field practice. In 1963 he received his PhD in political science from the University of São Paulo, Brazil.

From January 1964 to September 1965 Denis was under contract as a development adviser to USAID in Recife, Brazil. There he met and wooed (under the watchful eye of a chaperone) Ana Maria, a beautiful, vivacious Brazilian woman, who became the anchor of his life. Shortly thereafter he moved her from Recife to the University of Saskatchewan, Canada, testing a love that lasted over 40 years. Stops in Bloomington, Santa Barbara, San Diego, Cambridge, and Washington, D.C. finally led in 1979 to Notre Dame at the invitation of Fr. Hesburgh. The department of economics, the Peace Institute, and the Kellogg Institute were immeasurably enriched by his presence.

Denis often reflected on how useful it was to have lived with communities of struggle and communities of need, for longer or shorter periods, in France, Spain, Algeria, Lebanon, Brazil, Mexico, Peru, Sri Lanka, India, and elsewhere. Especially instructive to him were periods spent sharing the life of two nomadic tribes in the northern Sahara (1958), of indigenous peoples in the Brazilian Amazon (1961), and of Spanish Gypsies in Andalusia (1968). Simply living and working, not doing formal research, was essential for the development ethics field he was pioneering. As he says, "Development ethicists are, of necessity, selective consumers of findings from other disciplines, including the discipline known in Spanish as *la vivencia*—the living of life.

Denis's determination to emphasize justice in development, to put people at the center of decision-making, to insist on respect for cultural differences, and to challenge us to ethical commitment that recognized the equality of all peoples' rights everywhere formed the basis for the new field of development ethics.

One measure of Denis's importance in the field is that IDEA—the International Development Ethics Association— has established the Denis Goulet Prize in Development Ethics to be offered from time to time to an undergraduate or graduate student who submits a 4000-5000 word essay on a related topic. An international panel selects the winning entry. This is the only award given by IDEA.

## The Man

Denis was not only a scholar/practitioner but a man—a teacher/mentor/friend and husband/father. Let me read a few quotes from colleagues and students.

Let me start with a perceptive quote from Thomas Merton's journal, *Learning to Love*, Vol. 6, 1967: "Denis Goulet—from the U. of Indiana—was here the other day. A lovely young guy with a lot of good ideas—interested in development of 3rd world and the sociological-religious problems involved. But has a scientific capacity to deal with these things on a professional level. I envy him—he gets all over the place—got a doctorate in Brazil, married a Brazilian girl, involved in a cooperative in Patagonia, lived a while at the fraternity of the Little Brothers in the desert—at—El Abiod, worked in Algeria, Lebanon (?), Bolivia, stayed with some Indians in the Amazon jungle. ... Goulet is an interesting and worth while person, not a square, not contaminated by his professional milieu, honest, open, with ideas of his own and an intelligible speech." (April 26, 1967)

"I want again to express my personal gratitude for you, for your being, and for your doing. More than three decades ago, before I knew you as a personal friend, I read your work and was deeply influenced by it. In fact, it is no exaggeration to say that your path-breaking work on a normative theory of economic development changed my life and intellectual trajectory on the topic of development assistance." (Robert Johansen)

"...there is one type of human being that's even rarer...it's the one who has this powerful intellect, can talk your ears off and leave your brain throbbing, but who will also just as easily, just as effortlessly, just as naturally, approach one of his daughters, stroke her hair, take her face in his hands and smile into her eyes like he's beholding the greatest creation of all. Intellect, affection, love. All in one person, all to a profound level. Amazing." (student)

Denis was a man full of the love of life, a battler with a strong will. When he was dying in the hospital and his daughters Sinane and Andrea told him that his wife Ana Maria had spent the night in his hospital room, he said "I'm the luckiest man in the world." He often said to me during his last months that he couldn't be depressed about his illness because his Ana Maria wouldn't let him. She embraced life with gusto, and it kept him alive and filled with hope.

He also never lost his sense of humor. In the hospital his three women were around him singing. Denis's eyes seemed fixed on Ana Maria; he was calm and attentive. When they finished singing, Denis laboriously lifted his right hand, seemingly trying to reach for something. They tried to figure out what he wanted (his left arm and leg were paralyzed). They finally realized he wanted to clap for their singing, so they helped him clap. Later when told of his one-handed clapping, he replied (with much effort to be understood), "Only a Zen master can do that!"

Denis was a man of faith and his faith saw him through. Our trip (with Mike Garvey) a few years ago to the Trappist Abbey in Iowa demonstrated to us the importance of faith in Denis's life. On the lighter side Garvey and I marveled at Denis's driving while talking and waving his arms at the same time. It clearly was faith that got us there safe and sound. Once there, not only could Denis sink into the silence with reverence but astonishingly his normal flow of words slowed to a trickle while we were there. He already had the leukemia that eventually killed him, and his concentration and demeanor reflected an acceptance of whatever was to come. We often discussed this quote from scripture that we both loved: "I tell you, unless a grain of wheat falls into the earth and dies, it remains just a single grain; but if it dies, it bears much fruit."

# 15. Don McNeill, c.s.c.

I FIRST MET FR. DON MCNEILL in 1974 while we were still living in Washington, D.C. He came and spoke to Denis Goulet and me about his idea to transform Notre Dame's College of Arts and Letters into a College of Global Justice. The next year I came to Notre Dame as a faculty member. While Don's college idea didn't sell, the outcome was still exciting, the founding in 1983 of the Center for Social Concerns; in which I played a part, even if a minor one, from the beginning.

We became good friends with Don both as colleagues at the university and personally. Don started a group discussion he called the "mid-life crisis" group. We met once a month in people's homes, had dinner, and talked about where our lives were headed. It was a great group: Don, us, Claude Pomerleau, c.s.c., Ken & Penny Jameson, Lee & Sparky Tavis, Jim & Mary Ann Roemer. Our discussions were lively and valuable for this stage in our lives.

Let me give a flavor of who Don was by quoting from colleagues and former students on the occasion of his retirement:

> "Fr. Don has been a priest, mentor, and guide. As an undergraduate at Notre Dame and then a Holy Cross seminarian, Don revealed how to embrace a religious life which strives for justice. As I became a spouse and parent, Don encouraged me to pursue a life of washing the feet of others, without overlooking those closest in community. Living a vocation to apply the Catholic Social Tradition within institutions, Don delighted in walking the journey together. Gracias, Padre Don!"—*Bill Purcell, Center for Social Concerns*

> "Don McNeill is a man with many names: Fr. Don, Padre, Don Alto. For me, his names are also teacher of compassion, model of vulnerability, living gracias, and embracer of joy and suffering. I'm forever grateful to him and to God for the bountiful fruits of his life and friendship."—*Felicia Johnson O'Brien, Center for Social Concerns*

> "Father Don was a man that trusted people and saw their potential. He celebrated all of humanity across boundaries he helped to bridge. His support of the laity and for women's roles in the Church resonated widely, and his vision of what can be done to heal the world inspired students, faculty, alumni, and partners of all walks. Gracias Padre Don. Now it is up to us to carry on the work your life manifested."—*Jay Brandenberger, Center for Social Concerns*

> "Fr. Don taught and guided so many throughout his life to know the Compassionate God, to walk the Compassionate Life, and to practice the Compassionate Way. As students, friends, family and loved ones of Fr. Don's, let us say "Yes" to compassionate love, as a force for prayer and action, as expression of God's love for us that moves us to action for others. ¡Gracias por todo, Padre!"—*Rachel Tomas Morgan, Center for Social Concerns*

> "I am most grateful for the gift of Padre Don's life, for his witness, and for the deep gratitude that flowed from him. As is true for so many others, he changed the course of my life professionally, personally and sacramentally. It is my deep privilege to have worked with him at the Center for Social Concerns and to have called him friend, amigo, y Padre. I say ¡Gracias! for his life!"—*Annie Cahill Kelly, Center for Social Concerns*

The eulogy for Fr. Don, on his death at 81, captures the spirit of the man and his role of witness to so many:

A native of Chicago, Father McNeill was born on April 14, 1936, the second of the three sons of Donald and Katherine McNeill. His father and namesake was a pioneer radio personality, whose "Breakfast Club" variety show was the longest-running program in network radio history. A 1958 Notre Dame alumnus and a member of the Notre Dame faculty since 1966, Father McNeill was ordained a priest in the Congregation of Holy Cross in 1965, studied theology at the Pontifical Gregorian University in Rome and earned a doctoral degree from Princeton Theological Seminary in 1971.

On the rare occasions when Father McNeill could be persuaded to comment on a ministry and career that profoundly affected the institutional shape and mission of the University, he would speak less of his own role than those of three other Notre Dame priests—Rev. Theodore M. Hesburgh, C.S.C., the 15th president; Monsignor John Joseph Egan, the activist Chicago priest who assisted Father Hesburgh from 1970 to 1983; and Father Henri Nouwen, the spiritual writer and visiting lecturer in psychology at Notre Dame from 1966 to 1968.

His early years of teaching were challenging, he once confessed in an interview. When he returned from Rome to the Notre Dame campus, he had doubts that he "could be a teacher in the classical sense" and felt out of place. "I was feeling unqualified as far as my prayer life...and I didn't want to be a hypocrite," he said.

Father McNeill credited Father Nouwen and Father Hesburgh not only for strengthening his vocation, but also for encouraging and deepening his doctoral study of pastoral theology, which convinced him of the crucial importance of fusing experiential and interdisciplinary learning with religious faith. It was a conviction to which Father McNeill, in collaboration with Monsignor Egan, gave academic and institutional expression in numerous theology courses, community-based research projects and service learning immersions, which have since come to exemplify Notre Dame's commitment to the social teaching of the Catholic Church. It also gave rise to the 1981 book "Compassion: A Reflection on the Christian Life," which he co-authored with Father Nouwen and Douglas A. Morrison.[137]

Father McNeill also was one of a small number of priests in residence in Notre Dame's first women's residence halls. He continually advocated for greater involvement of women and laity in the Church and acknowledged the women he considered spiritual mentors in the later days of his life.

Father McNeill's devotion to his students and to Catholic social teaching made him one of Notre Dame's most popular and influential teachers. A faculty award citation in 1980 described how "with his large frame

*and larger vision, he moves in and out of the lives of students and faculty,*
*probing, seeking and challenging - reminding us all that education can*
*never be contained totally in the lecture hall, the library or the laboratory.*
*He dreams about this place in the great tradition of his predecessors in*
*Holy Cross.*

*In 1983, one of the fondest of Father McNeill's dreams was realized in*
*the establishment of Notre Dame's Center for Social Concerns, of which*
*Father McNeill served as executive director until 2002. Committed to*
*engaged learning, research and service informed by the Catholic social*
*tradition, the center is a crucial and distinctive component of a Notre*
*Dame education and involves more than 2,500 students annually in its*
*programs.*[138]

"Father Don had a vision of Notre Dame students not just
learning but enacting the Catholic social tradition through
compassionate care for those on the margins," said Rev. Paul
Kollman, C.S.C., Leo and Arlene Hawk Executive Director
of the Center for Social Concerns. "By joining theological reflection with research and learning that is grounded in community partnerships, he established a foundation for the Center for Social Concerns that has guided us ever after."

Don was a large man, 6'8", and during the last 20+ years
he suffered from severe neck and back pains. Despite these
being debilitating at times, he refused to allow them to derail
his life and work. He not only founded the Center for Social
Concerns, but he was its director for many years. After retiring
from that he became an assistant pastor in a Hispanic Chicago
parish. When the pain became too intense, he returned to
Notre Dame to live at the Holy Cross assisted living house.
Even then he was still available for a friendly word, informal
counseling, or just a great smile.

## 16. Ralph & Reggie Weissert

BEFORE MOVING TO SOUTH BEND, a friend from our CFM group in Washington said, "you have to look up the Weissert's; they are great people and pioneers in CFM." Among the first people we sought out after moving was the Weissert's. It was a match made in Heaven. We became close friends. Together we started a CFM group and were two of the four couples that started the Holy Family Catholic Worker House. Reggie frequently had us over for dinner when she had out of town company. We met wonderful folks this way—Patty Crowley, Rose Lucey, priests from around the world, and too many others to remember. We knew Reggie better than Ralph because he died much too early at age 70 while Reggie kept going until she was 95, passing away on March 31, 2015.

Reggie's parents, her husband Ralph, Fr. Louis Putz and the Christian Family Movement were the major influences in her life. Members of Little Flower Parish, she and Ralph belonged to CFM, serving on the National and International Coordinating Committees. She introduced their family to the wider world by welcoming international students to the family through international student programs. In the late 60's, Reggie was involved with the local paper "The Reformer," a local African American newspaper, and served on the Panel of American Women.

From 1973-1980, she ran the summer program for Notre Dame's Catholic Committee on Urban Ministry, and later worked at Notre Dame's Center for Social Concern. Over the years, she served on the boards of Planned Parenthood, the United Religious Community and the Catholic Worker House. She volunteered at the Center for the Homeless and St. Augustine's Soup Kitchen and was an active member of Call to Action. In 2004, when she was 81, Reggie initiated the local Interfaith Women's Dialogue Group (for Christians, Jews and Muslims) with Rihab Quddoura, firmly believing that dialogue is crucial for people to bring about peace. Reggie showed us all how to keep-on going, advancing age was no excuse.

In May 2014, Charlie Kenny, a Notre Dame student from the 1970s who knew Reggie from the Urban Plunge, ran into Reggie when he went to dinner with his parents. His encounter with her prompted these reflections, which he shared upon her death.

### Reggie's Hands
*Reggie's hands, warm and strong*
*lead me to the water, quickening.*
*Reggie's eyes, warm and clear*
*see what mine do not.*
*Reggie's voice, warm and soft,*
*welcomes me home*
*to good people,*
*good people, we say,*
*Don and Fran and Doug*
*good people, the edges of life melting away,*
*living memories remaining.*

*Her frailness strengthens me,*
*her hands sustaining.*
*"If you pray," she laughs gently, "pray for Joe."*
*Good people welcome me home.*
*My father's hands, longer, bonier,*
*embrace mine.*
*Mom's hands, busy, sharing, serving,*
*good people*

## 17. Michael & Margaret Garvey

WE MET THE GARVEY'S shortly after they moved to South Bend in the early 1980s. Michael started a job in public relations at Notre Dame and Margaret was caring for two young sons. We have been close friends for over 35 years. If I had to use one word that most reflects their lives it would be hospitality. Their house always seems open to welcome friends, relatives, strangers, and even a parade of dogs with saintly names such as Basil.

A few years ago, when Michael's father died (his mother had died earlier), his oldest sibling (there are eight), who was executor, decided that in order of age each should choose something they wanted from the house. The oldest chose the dining room and chairs, that seat 12, and said "I am giving this to Michael and Margaret because they are the most hospitable in the family". The second oldest sibling chose a huge wall mounted sculpture of the Last Supper and said, "I am giving this to Michael and Margaret because they are most like our parents were extending hospitality." The table and chairs and the sculpture are now front and center in their dining room and get constant use.

Their whole life has been dedicated to providing hospitality. They, we and two other couples founded the Holy Family Catholic Worker House in South Bend in 1985, that ran for almost 20 years. Margaret, when their now three children reached school age, started working at Logan Center that serves mentally challenged men and women from the community.

Their past activities are even more demonstrative of their hospitality. Margaret Quigley Garvey founded the Davenport, Iowa Catholic Worker House in the mid-1970s and ran it for seven years. Michael lived and worked there for three years where they met and eventually married.[139]

Reminiscing about those days running the Davenport House, Margaret said: "I think there is a lot of drama about hospitality. I did the dramatic stuff for a long time. For seven years. Loved every minute of it, but I wouldn't have the energy now to do what I did then. The first year, we would have fifty people a night sleeping on the floor. And then after a lot of violence (and we had a lot of violence), we cut back. One of our staff was beaten up with a railroad tie. And we all agreed we couldn't let people keep coming in droves."[140]

A staff member of the house, Charles Walzem, speaking about Margaret, said: "That Margaret Garvey. She was special all right! In some Catholic Worker houses, you have people who are willing to care for just one person and Margaret did a whole lot of that. She bathed these old guys, she clothed them, she fed them in their beds if they were dying. Margaret was extraordinary. Her vitality, her…just her sense of loving the poor. It was there."[141]

In 2014, Robert M. Coughlin, remembered back on his days working at Margaret's house in Davenport:

*I lived at the Catholic Worker house in Davenport, Iowa, in the summer of 1976. Margaret Quigley Garvey was the founder and leader of that house. She and her husband Mike Garvey have published books on*

*Dorothy and the Catholic Worker. That summer has influenced my entire adult life.*

*Currently I work at a meal for the hungry and homeless at St. Mary church in Painesville, Ohio. The program, called the Karpos Ministry, was established five years ago by Kathy Philipps and a seminarian friend of hers. Hard to say how many people help put on these meals twice a week (serving up to 200 meals per night). The regular helpers number about 20, with another 10-15 coming occasionally.*

*The Spirit of the Catholic Worker and its mission to live out the Works of Mercy is alive and well!*[142]

Michael Garvey's short memoir[143] of his time working in the Davenport Catholic Worker House became a required read in my home. My daughter, Alice, spent a weekend volunteering there and came home with Michael's book. This experience led her to volunteer for a year with the Glenmary project in Rock Hill, South Carolina, during the JP Stevens boycott.

The book consists of a series of short chapters describing his experiences with a group of remarkable guests with colorful names such as Three-Finger Floyd, Loretta the Exorcist and Pete Domino. He doesn't romanticize or demonize them; they come across as real people, complete with blemishes but great holiness as well. That is the point of the memoir, as well as of all his writing; seeing Christ in everyone. Michael understands Dorothy Day's difficult dictum: "I really only love God as much as I love the person I love the least."

Michael continued to turn out an almost endless supply of short essays for a variety of venues including the National Catholic Reporter. They always displayed his rock-solid commitment to his Catholic faith if not always to its leaders. Both he and Margaret exemplified Dorothy Day's lifelong commitment to traditional Catholic values and radical social action. A reviewer of Michael's Confessions book Writes:

*Garvey admits on several occasions to weariness, spiritual and physical. Sometimes he confesses that he simply wants to run away from the grime and odors of the Catholic Worker House and find himself a quiet place in a nice neighborhood. At other times Garvey is uncomfortably aware that he has a safety net that makes his voluntary poverty very complicated indeed. "There's one tension at this place that is...irreconcilable. We (the staff workers) have chosen to be here... For all our attempts to identify with the poor and the weak, we will never share with them the involuntary nature of their poverty." (92) But he's clearly a guy so aflame with Jesus' revolutionary Gospel that occasional despair and doubt feed rather than deplete him. The honesty with which he sometimes questions the course he's chosen is refreshing and makes his story even more gripping.*[144]

For years Michael and I have had lunch together about once a month. We discuss everything but almost always end up talking about how you act in the secular world as a believing Catholic. We often disagree on details, such as he focuses more on abortion and I on the balance of positions a politician takes. Both Michael and Margaret have been ongoing sources of inspiration as companions on the Way.

# 18. Bill Toohey, c.s.c.

FR. BILL TOOHEY was head of campus ministry at the University of Notre Dame when I joined the faculty in 1975. He did the 9:30am Mass every Sunday at Sacred Heart Church on campus. Our family quickly chose to make that our weekly mass. Bill was the best homilist I have ever heard. Every sermon was at root about love. God is love, we are called to love, no exceptions. He had great ability to translate all the new theology coming out of the reforms initiated by Vatican II.

Bill used this focus on a God of love to explain what it means that Jesus died for our sins. This had always bothered me. Why did a good God require the death of his own son as expiation for our sins? Listen to Bill from a sermon printed in his book, *Born Alive.*

## Way of the Cross

*Although the gory details of the Way of the Cross have been made the central point by a thousand preachers, they are truly incidental to the discovery that the important thing was that Jesus was obedient to the Father, accepting whatever was going to come his way, with free men acting freely. The Father had no desire for his son to die on the cross. The fact that he had decided to allow man to be free does not at all mean he wished free men to so misuse their freedom that they slaughtered his son.*

*Jesus did what he did, not so that the Father would relent and relinquish his grudge, but so that we would relent. He did it so that we would relent now from our violence (revealed in a God of love hung on a tree); and so that we would relent from our resistance to the Father who calls us to himself. That is how Jesus saves us "through his death on the cross." He would save us from missing the whole meaning of life; from giving ourselves to the wrong god; from our blindness to the loving appeals of a God so amazing he loves us even when we kill his son.*

Unfortunately, Bill died in 1980 from encephalitis. He made such an impact on us and on so many others that in 2005 we held a 25th memorial service at his gravesite.

# 19. John Gerber, c.s.c.

I MET JOHN GERBER in the 1970s but didn't get to know him well until the later 1980s when he invited us to join his prayer group called The Quiet Place. We met once a month at the married students social center for a meal and prayer and reflection. The group was mainly academics, which meant a tendency to talk-talk and become abstract and philosophical. John brought us back to earth with his deeply-felt personal reflections that made you really focus on the spiritual meaning of a scripture passage or on what someone in the group had said in a less than clear way.

When John died in 1995, his Wake, held at Moreau Seminary, showed me that John was much more than an academic. The room was filled with priests, faculty in suits, and lots of men in shirt sleeves with tattoos. It turns out that John had been an alcoholic and entering recovery became the chaplain for AA in South Bend. Again, a lesson learned. Do not judge by appearances.

Shortly before he died John sent a letter to his friends that I have presented below. It shows the spiritual depth of this wonderful man.

1 March 1995
Ash Wednesday

Dear Chuck & Mary Ellen

Since December 9, when I began the first of two week-long stays in the hospital, I've done scarcely any correspondence except for the Christmas cards I got out shortly after that. Meanwhile Christmas and New Years have come and gone and cards and letters have piled up, yours among them. Please excuse me for not having gotten back to you long since. Believe me, I am most grateful for your concern, support and prayers. I write now aware that we are entering upon Lent, the season in which we try most intently to live the mystery of Jesus' dying and rising.

During these two months and more, I have been occupied with learning how to live in my new situation, first in the hospital while being treated for blood clots in my legs, and since December 24 in Holy Cross House, the C.S.C. infirmary just across one of the Notre Dame lakes from the University campus. From about mid-November until a month ago, I was receiving weekly chemotherapy treatments. At that time, the oncologist had to inform me that the chemo was not effective and that all medicine could now offer was attention to the effects of the disease and to comfort. Holy Cross House is an ideal setting for this, and I am grateful to be here under the care of a wonderful nursing staff and amid forty of my Holy Cross colleagues, many of whom have been in years past my teachers and mentors. I am living with my spiritual fathers and grandfathers!

《《《《《《《《《

I am very conscious that I am dying and that my essential inner task now is to live this death and birth with grateful and reverent attention to what God is giving me in this privileged time. By God's grace I am able to feel that this is the path I am invited to walk—that in God's mysterious and loving providence the essential tasks of my life are completed, it is not necessary for me to live any longer, and that I am being summoned toward the Presence I have yearned for since boyhood and which I have tried to serve and celebrate. I have nothing but gratitude for my life and, while I would be willing to live longer, I am at peace that God is offering me a new way.

At the same time, I have scarcely begun to know how painful it is going to be to part from so many dear people—family. Community and other friends—as well as from this blessed and troubled but always dear earth, and to suffer in this illness that sundering of body from spirit through which one is born to resurrection. For that reason, I ask your continued remembrance and prayers, and I assure you of mine now and later. I assure you, too, of my affection and gratitude for your presence in my life and for your goodness to me. If you do not hear from me again, know that that is because of incapacity, not because of lack of caring.

In the Life of the Crucified and Risen One,<br>
John Gerber, C.S.C.

*Highlighting the spiritual aura that shone through his life and death, John died at high noon (literally) on Easter Sunday, 1995.*

# 20. Jim Langford

The Times of My Life
Jim Langford

I MET JIM LANGFORD almost 40 years ago. In 1983, as the Director of the University of Notre Dame Press, he published my book, co-authored with Ken Jameson, A*n Inquiry into the Poverty of Economics.* He went on to publish in 1990 our follow up book, *Beyond Reaganomics: A Further Inquiry into the Poverty of Economics.* In fact, Jim was the one who came up with the *Poverty of Economics* title. We had started with a boring academic title that was too long to run on one line or even two.

What has most impressed me about Jim is his capability in a variety of areas. He has been a first-rate publisher, at University of Michigan Press, University of Notre Dame Press, and Corby Press. He has overseen the publication of over 1000 books. He has authored many books himself[145] while, at the same time, teaching the Core Course at Notre Dame; which is a form of modern great books program.

Finally, I come to Jim's activity that impresses me the most. Actually, it overwhelms me with its creativity, its importance, and the amount of effort involved. Jim, with his then wife,[146]

Jill, had moved south of the city to a place with acreage, to get away, for peace and quiet. That was the year Jim's core course was reading *There Are No Children Here*, by Alex Kotlowitz, a visiting professor of American studies at Notre Dame. The book details the lives of two inner-city children in Chicago's Henry Horner projects; children whose childhood is lost in a blur of the neighborhood's frequent gunfights and drug deals. That's when Jim started dinnertime discussions with Jill about turning their 16-acre property into an area where disadvantaged children can be children and play. The result is best told in an article titled with the name the Langford's gave their project, *There are Children Here*.

## There are Children Here

Jill and James Langford laugh when they talk about buying their expansive grounds in the country, a few miles south of Notre Dame. "We moved out there to be private—to get away from it all," says Jim '59, an adjunct assistant professor in ND's core course and former director of Notre Dame Press. Jill '80, the owner of publishing company Diamond Communications, nods in agreement. "We had moved out here to do our own thing," she says, "and felt a bit selfish."

Step outside their house, with its airy floor plan, and the shouts of children drown out any semblance of privacy or selfishness or getting away from it all. There are children playing basketball on an asphalt court in front of a set of bleachers. There are children giggling on a swing set. There are children building castles in the sand pit, children heading into a small clubhouse, children on the baseball diamond, children climbing a wooden playhouse, children talking, children riding bikes, children, children everywhere.

Only two of them are Langford children. The rest, about

20 on this sunny spring afternoon, are part of the "There Are Children Here" day camp run by the Langford's on their country property in Lakeville. Keeping an eye on the free-flowing activities are several volunteers, most of them Notre Dame students.

In the midst of it all are Jill and Jim, who appreciate the irony of the trip they made from seeking privacy to seemingly never having a moment's peace. The Langford's adopted Trevor in 1990 and moved to the expansive property in 1993, the same year they adopted Emily.

Their own two children are biracial, and Trevor is learning-challenged, notes Jim. "Dealing with him and his problems put us in touch with a lot of different people," he says. What the Langford's discovered was that disadvantaged children in South Bend also are often limited in what they can do for fun. "The kids can't go to Muessel Park," he says about a park near downtown South Bend. "There are drugs sold there."

Taking a deep breath, the couple built a baseball diamond on their lot and opened the camp in 1994. Since then the Langford's have added a clubhouse, with a kitchen where snacks are prepared and a fireplace for group reading sessions; a little theater building for impromptu theatricals; a basketball court; sand pit; and a variety of other play spaces. Biking trails meander through the nearby woods.

During the school year, local children ages 4 to 11 from seven different groups (such as the local Boys & Girls Club), can be found at the camp from 4 to 6 p.m. four days a week. "There's a core of 150 to 200 kids who come here often," says Jim. Over the summer, the camp is open from 9:30 a.m. to 4:30 p.m., five days a week, again for children recommended by local groups and centers. Two or three paid staff members assist during the summer.

In case that doesn't sound busy enough, the Langford's added something new a few years ago. Now, about six or seven times a year, the camp brings in Latino and African-American children from parochial schools in Chicago, sponsored by the Inner-City Teaching Corps. Those campers take the South Shore to South Bend on Friday night, sleep over in the camp's clubhouse, take a tour of Notre Dame on Saturday and hop back onto the train Saturday evening.

"We just play with them; let the kids be kids," says Marissa Moschel, a Notre Dame sophomore. She particularly likes that there is no organized schedule of activities; when the children arrive they are free to join any group or activity they wish. "That's the fun of it," she says.

"It's as much fun for the students as it is for the kids," says Maura Malloy '02, who worked during the summer program last year. "It gets rid of some stress of studying."

Stress is something the Langford's hope to ease for the campers, too. "A lot of these kids are really afraid," says Jill, who occasionally does a quick batch of laundry when a day camper is scared to go home because his clothes are dirty. "They get shouted at all the time," adds Jim, who encourages volunteers to keep that fact in mind.

The few rules of the camp are not arbitrary, says Jim, and are explained to the children when they arrive. "The desire to teach them to make good decisions never changes," he says.

The camp also helps dispel one gnawing problem. "They're always hungry," says Jill. Snacks are constantly available in the clubhouse, and the children are sent home with a packed bag of food. The children frequently share their food bags with siblings, Jill notes. "We find a lot of that—how much they care for each other."

One thing the Langford's also found was how difficult it

is for them to say farewell at the end of each camping session. "We wanted to adopt about every other one," says Jill. The Langford's also have learned that social justice projects don't come cheap or easy. "Teaching social justice is one thing," says Jim, "But to do it..."

Insurance eats up a third of the camp's yearly $22,000 budget. The presence of hate groups in the area means no sign identifies the location of the camp. And Jim himself has opted to avoid the route of grants and public funding, preferring to stump for private donations instead. An endowment, says Jim, "would take the edge off of it."

And yes, there is another price; mainly, says Jill, fatigue. Then the kids and the volunteers arrive, and the organized chaos begins. "We've never questioned why we did it," says Jill, who's so energetic she can barely sit still. "I have relied on grace to persevere," says Jim, whose heart surgery last year has forced him to slow down a bit. "This has brought my faith alive."[147]

Jim loves Notre Dame, the Chicago Cubs, books, and the doing of justice. A witness par excellence. A wonderful companion on the Way.

## 21. Michael Baxter

I HAVE KNOWN MICHAEL BAXTER for some 20 years in a variety of capacities. We are friends, have been colleagues at Notre Dame, fellows of the Peace Institute, and officers on the board of the Catholic Worker affiliated Our Lady of the Road Café and Drop-In Center.

Michael developed a widespread reputation as a teacher of undergraduates at Notre Dame. I know this from several sources. Faculty members in Theology have told me that they hear from their students that Michael is an inspiring teacher who is also demanding of good performance on the students' part. I have taught a number of students who have had Michael previously and they rave about his courses, particularly the one entitled "A Faith to Die For." My own observation is that they show a sophisticated understanding of their faith in my course on Catholic Social Thought and the U.S. Economy. Finally, each year I asked Michael to make a presentation to my class and he did a wonderful job of engaging the students.

My involvement in theology has been focused on the nexus between theological perspectives and their bearing on

Catholic social thought, particularly in economics. With this background, I have come to appreciate the perspective Michael has brought to the field of Catholic social ethics and have come to see Baxter's work as important for judging the challenges facing the Church regarding teaching on economics. I have read a number of Michael's articles and they have been very helpful in understanding the different strands of the Catholic tradition, particularly in understanding how the philosophy of the Catholic Worker fits into that tradition. Michael's critique of the policy approach has become more persuasive to me in recent years. I have incorporated his ideas into my research on the contrast between Baxter's prophetic approach and Fr. Bryan Hehir's public church approach as argued in Kristin Heyer's, *Prophetic and Public: The Social Witness of U.S. Catholicism.*

Michael is truly both an academic and an activist. It is not enough for him to teach and write about building a truly human and Christian community, he actively attempts to put his faith and work into action. His work in co-founding the Peter Claver Catholic Worker House here in South Bend has been amazing. Everybody, including me, told him to go slow and be cautious. Michael plunged ahead, raised the funds, bought a house, then another and another. He has three houses for homeless men, women, and even families. The money came in as needed (Michael knows how to touch those who might contribute). And then he went out and rented a huge building, an old lumber yard, and converted it into a place for the homeless to get out of the cold in winter and heat in summer, get a shower, wash their clothes, and get a bite to eat. The wonderfully named Our Lady of the Road has been a great success and provided a vitally needed service. Even more impressive, Michael formed and developed a community of people who now do that work, a community of 10 or so, plus an extended community of scores of volunteers who operate Our Lady of the Road drop-in center and support the houses.

Michael has done an excellent job of integrating Notre Dame students into the Catholic Worker operations. Many students have come from campus at his behest and gotten involved. Michael spoke to one of my classes about his idea for a homeless run cooperative called Miraculous Metals to collect metal cans and whatever for sale to recycling plants with the proceeds paying salaries and the profit used to run the drop-in center. One of my students took up Michael's ideas for his term paper and made part of the project the organization of can collecting in his dorm which then went to the Catholic Worker. This was successful for three years with each year the project passed on to a new group of students. Then the university took over the project hiring a recycling company.

Michael found that after 25 years as a Holy Cross priest he couldn't continue. He needed intimacy. Leaving Notre Dame and teaching at DePaul in Chicago, he eventually moved to Denver, got married, had two children, and teaches at Regis College. Despite the changes the flame still burns. While writing theology articles and teaching he looks to start a Catholic Worker farm in the Denver area.

One of Michael's Notre Dame students wrote a Tribute upon his leaving Notre Dame:

> In a pair of black jeans, work boots and a button-down flannel shirt with the sleeves rolled up, Michael Baxter is right at home. Although for the casual observer it might be difficult to tell exactly where that home is.
>
> Having spent the last 30 years sojourning across the country and living in all manner of places, from the Holy Cross novitiate in the mountains of Colorado Springs, to teaching and studying at great universities like Duke, Notre Dame and Princeton, to living in humble church rectories or Catholic Worker houses, most recently in a modest apartment across the street from the St. Peter Claver Catholic Worker, a house dedicated to

serving the poor and homeless of South Bend that he co-founded in 2003, Michael Baxter's home is not where he lays his head at night.

When I first met Michael Baxter '83M.Div., I was a freshman at Notre Dame and he was a Holy Cross priest and theology professor, living on West Washington Street in South Bend, the site of the original Peter Claver Catholic Worker. With its dilapidated front porch and haggard garden, the house was welcoming but in poor shape.

Baxter, as he's often affectionately called, slept on a futon mattress on the floor, in a house with bullet holes still in the walls. His Notre Dame salary and donations helped keep the place running. While he didn't seem to own much, he valued what he did have: his books, four sweaters, religious icons, Bruce Springsteen and Neil Young records. Of course we, his students, counted, too. He shared a bathroom, meals and common life with a revolving cast of homeless folks and student characters, and he didn't hesitate to ask a kid who'd grown up in a nice house in a safe neighborhood and aced her SATs, to leave the security of campus for a few hours to help out and get to know some poor people, all the while giving her a hard time for not knowing how to use a hammer or a coffee percolator.

Baxter was just as at home sharing a meal with someone right out of prison as he was jogging around the lakes in front of Moreau or blasting the Lonesome Dove soundtrack in his pick-up truck. He was just as at ease delivering a paper at an academic conference as he was ministering to soldiers or saying Mass in Dillon Hall, where he lived in residence for four years.

Michael Baxter was a radical, even disruptive presence in the lives of his students simply because he attempted to live as if the gospel mattered. He had a way of drawing people in. ND students came in droves every Thursday night for Milkshake Mass in Dillon Hall. They came to hear life-changing homilies delivered in the famous Baxter whisper, to stand around after Mass and ask him questions, to have their consciences pricked and prodded, to hear the gospel as if for the first time. He made us question all our stuff, and with it, our allegiances and priorities.

Michael Baxter's radical Catholicism, hospitality, availability and sense of humor brought students together who ordinarily would have been strangers to one another. His classes attracted liberals and conservatives, the greatest doubters and the most devout. In one of Baxter's legendary courses, "A Faith to Die For," it was not uncommon to see kids from all over the political and theological spectrum, from Young Republicans, Campus Ministry and Children of Mary types, to the Progressive Student Alliance, Center *for Social Concerns and Ultimate Frisbee crowd. His courses on war and peace attracted members of both ROTC and Pax Christi USA.*

*This is in part because Michael Baxter doesn't call home one of the established theological camps. He's worked to stake out his own position, which at best finds its home in the pilgrim community of the Catholic Worker. He is neither conservative nor liberal; in some ways, he's both. He opposes abortion, the death penalty, euthanasia and all war. He is often lumped in intellectually with his friend and mentor Stanley Hauerwas, and yet his affinities with thinkers like Germain Grisez or Ralph McInerny, his good friend who is now deceased, betray openness to the natural law that would almost certainly make Hauerwas cringe.*

*And while he's written scores of scholarly articles and delivered as many papers, his forthcoming book, God, Notre Dame, Country: Rethinking the Mission of Catholic Higher Education in the United States and other projects always seem to take second place to his relationships with people. When I visited other professors' offices as a student, it was always to ask a question about an assignment, but I often stopped by Professor Baxter's office in Malloy Hall just to talk. He had a way of making you feel welcome, like he'd been hoping you'd pop in. His office was always a mess of books and papers, floor to ceiling, and on every available surface, and certainly he had work to do. But he always made you feel like you were his top priority. He'd be in the midst of writing when I'd knock, and as soon as I walked in the door he'd drop everything, shove some books off a footstool and offer me a place to sit.*

*How did he ever get any work done? If he was in a rush or on his way to a meeting he'd say, "Walk with me," and listen to your problem all the way there. Other professors went home, but Baxter was always available to his students, friends and those in need.*

*After spending 20 years as a Holy Cross priest (he officially left the priesthood in 2006), 15 as a member of the Notre Dame theology faculty, and eight as a co-founder and resident of the South Bend Catholic Worker, the second Catholic Worker he co-founded—the first being Andre House in Phoenix, Arizona—Michael Baxter is moving on from Notre Dame this fall. Still, this pilgrim soul and master teacher will be in his element, as his home is ultimately wherever his students are. After more than 30 years of teaching, serving, scholarship and causing a commotion in the academe and elsewhere, his students are everywhere.*

*Mike Baxter's legacy at Notre Dame and in South Bend ultimately resides in the lives he forever changed by giving someone a place to stay when they were living on the street with their children, or counseling a student in need, even in the middle of the night, or helping a graduate student with his dissertation. His former students are now moms and dads, priests and nuns, peace activists and fighter pilots, and yet they can each tell you what he taught them and how he challenged them.*

*Professor Baxter won't be at Notre Dame this fall to implore another class of students to practice the works of mercy and to protest war and injustice, or to inspire them with the lives of such American Catholics as Peter Maurin and Dorothy Day. Yet, Michael Baxter's remarkable life and sense of being rooted in God and the Church, despite his transience in space, reminds us that for the Catholic Christian, home is ultimately not a place at all but a practice.*

by Anna Keating

That is a tough act to follow. However, I need to say, what I said at the beginning of this memoir, it is Michael who pushed me to put down in writing Mary Ellen's and my experiences. Michael's example helps keep me humble. It is another among many such examples of how unrecognized witnesses are making this a better world.

## 22. Jim Burtchaell, c..s.c.

JIM BURTCHAELL became an important person in my life's journey. I first met him after I was hired by the University of Notre Dame. He was Provost of the university. It turns out that my wife, Mary Ellen, knew him and his family. They grew up a few blocks apart in the Laurelhurst Section of Portland, Oregon. As provost, Jim was seen as a tyrant by some and as a savior of the Catholic character of the university by others.

I got to know him, at first, through my wife. She invited him to lunch on a regular basis, particularly after he was fired as provost. In 1995 we were part of his biblical tour to the Holy Land and Assisi, Italy. There were 17 of us, all old friends or family members of his. This was a lifetime experience. Scripture came alive as we stopped and prayed on the Lake of Galilee, on the road to Jericho, the Garden of Olives, etc.

Over the years I learned much from and was stimulated by Jim's writings, particularly *Philemon's Problem* (1973). Introducing the book's topic, Paul asking Philemon to accept back his slave, Onesimus, as a brother, Jim wrote:

*I began again with Philemon, an earnest man troubled by a command that gave him no rest, yet offered peace. He was offered a gospel that he could not quite master. He responded, one trusts, to a summons that drew from him never enough, but more and more, much more even than he had planned to give or thought himself able to give. It transfigured him. It put nails through him. It was worth it. This book strains after what drew him on.*

Many years later (2011) Jim wrote: "Embarking on my 77th year of life and my 51st year as a Holy Cross priest, how grateful I am even still to be so drawn." Jim helped teach me to be grateful to be so challenged and drawn.

Jim was no saint, as few are. His flaws were deep and serious. But there was no question that his love of God was the inspiration that allowed him to go on with his journey, his pilgrimage. Late in life Alzheimer's disease took over his life. He came to his friends in the early stages and told them what lie ahead for him. He gave away all his possessions and entered the care of Holy Cross House on campus. He accepted this life without complaint. The night he died, the Garvey's, the Moriarty's, and us, hoisted farewell glasses of wine to a comatose Jim. He was dead by morning.

Nicholas Ayo, c.s.c., gave the eulogy at Jim's funeral in 2015:

*Fr. Burtchaell and I were roommates in the ground-floor room of Old College closest to the Log Chapel. We were both preparing to enter Holy Cross Novitiate in Jordan, Minnesota at the end of our freshman year at Notre Dame, which was the same year when the late Fr. Hesburgh was appointed University President. I remember well how my classmate knew Latin, and I did not. I remember well wandering the woods with Jim near the old Moreau Seminary, where we were looking for wild flowers to decorate a May Altar dedicated to Our Lady, Notre Dame. In the Novitiate we were together in the tailor-shop, the two tailors who could keep a cassock going long past its time on earth. Upon graduating from Notre Dame we were together in the Holy Cross group who boarded a ship to Rome, for theological studies prior to ordination to the priesthood. In subsequent years our paths diverged, he to Notre Dame and I to the University of Portland.*

*In Shakespeare's play, "Julius Caesar," Mark Anthony says: "I come to bury Caesar, not to praise him. The evil that men do lives after them. The good is oft interred with their bones." In our Catholic funerals such advice is never bad advice. The homily at the mass is not intended to be a eulogy, but a reflection on the Gospel in which we hope to connect the life of the deceased with the life of the crucified Christ.*

*Tonight, I want to speak to you of kings. Consider "Oedipus the King," an ancient tale so often told that fragile written texts was numerous enough to allow a few copies to survive the ravages of the ages. Oedipus' identity is concealed shortly after his birth and escape from an assassination plot. He grows up not knowing who he really is, and one might add, who fully does. In a quarrel he mistakenly kills a man who turns out to be his father, the king, and he marries the queen, who is his mother. When he discovers who he really is, he puts out his eyes in shame and guilt. And of us Jesus says on the cross: "Father, forgive them for they know not what they do."*

*I want to speak of the king who in the Bible overshadows the many centuries before Jesus. King David was talented in warfare and talented in politics. No one did more to expand and secure the territory that became Israel. But, king though he was, he took another man's wife and had her husband killed. David then became the model of repentance. Nevertheless, his household fell apart, ending with his Son trying to take his life. And yet, we so love David. He cared, and he owned his sin. "That man is you," says Nathan the prophet to David. And David knows now who he is, a great king and a great sinner, as to one degree or another remain the rest of us. Jesus came to us as the promised Messiah and our redeemer. He is announced as one of the "house of David," as proclaimed by the angel Gabriel to Mother Mary.*

*In medieval lore King Arthur and the knights of the round-table would establish equality in the kingdom and rule in peace ever after. However, the King's right-hand man, Lancelot, and the King's wife cannot keep from taking a corner at the round table. Camelot, just as the Garden of Paradise, proved to be all too vulnerable. And yet, such an ideal lives on in us all, and all the good we do in our lives is not cancelled out by our weakness and sin.*

*Tonight, in this church of God, let us now talk of the King of Kings, the Lord Jesus, over whose crucified head on the Calvary cross Pontius Pilate tacked up the inscription: "Jesus of Nazareth, King of the Jews." Dying alongside Jesus was a man usually described as a thief ( identified as a "revolutionary" in the present Lectionary). He acknowledges that he is a sinner who deserves his punishment, but he asks Jesus: "Remember me when you come into your kingdom." And Jesus, despite his own pain, with tender care promises: "This day you will be with me in paradise." Every one of us will be crucified in some way by life on earth. We all can say those same words to the Lord of life: "Remember me." Fr. Burtchaell suffered on a cross that took his brilliant mind from him many years before his time. He hung on that cross in his own unspoken agony with a patience that shames the smaller troubles most of us are plagued with. I can think of no better summary of the life of Jim Burtchaell, my roommate of our salad days, then to say I believe that he heard the same words Jesus spoke to that repentant human being in such pain crucified beside Jesus: "This day you will be with me in Paradise."*

## 23. Rashied Omar

I FIRST MET RASHIED when he entered the M.A. Program in Peace Studies at Notre Dame for the 2001-02 academic year. At that time, I was the graduate director for the Kroc Institute for International Peace Studies. Rashied arrived with his wife and five children from Cape Town, South Africa. I got to know Rashied quite well over the next few years. His family hosted one of my granddaughters at their mosque to help her fulfill a class assignment to learn about a religion other than her own. He also spent an evening talking to our prayer group about Islam and the Koran. Just a year ago he hosted several of my children and grandchildren in his home in South Africa.

Rashied went on to earn a PhD in religious studies from the University of Cape Town, He is now a member of the core faculty at the Kroc Institute. During Notre Dame's spring semester, he teaches a popular course on the Islamic ethics of war and peace as well as peace studies courses. For the remainder of the year, he serves as field research advisor to Kroc Institute's master's students in Cape Town, South Africa. In addition to his university-work, Rashied serves as Imam (religious minister) at the Claremont Main Road Mosque in Cape

Town, South Africa, a trustee of the Healing of Memories Institute in South Africa, a member of the Interfaith Council for Ethics Education, Arigatou International in Japan, and an advisory board member for Critical Investigations into Humanitarianism in Africa.

I learned from Rashied that Muslims, like Christians and Jews, were working to enhance their faith with an emphasis on justice and peace. Let me quote Rashied:

> *1976 was a year of major uprising in South Africa. There was an attempt by the apartheid government to impose the Afrikaans language as a medium of instruction. On 16 June 1976, students in a black township near Johannesburg called Soweto, protested against this imposition, and the police shot and killed some of the demonstrators. That sparked student demonstrations all over the country. I was a student leader in my school at the time. I led the student protest at my school and got imprisoned. I was suspended from school, put on trial, and lost a whole year as a result of this turmoil.*
>
> *Two things happened as a result of this experience in 1976. One, I became much more committed as an anti-apartheid activist to struggle for peace and justice. Second, I became much more spiritual and religious, because during this difficult time, I could draw on my own inner resources to sustain myself at that very young age. Since then, what I have tried to do is to build a bridge, to find a synthesis between spirituality and the struggle for peace and justice. The answer to how to combine these two in a healthy way lies in commitment to the core values of justice, "embracing the other" and compassion.*
>
> *Having been born and raised in South Africa, my own journey and struggle for justice in the anti-apartheid context has left an indelible impact in my life. After justice comes the notion of, what I would call, embracing the other. For me, the litmus test of a good religion, a good ideology or a world view is the extent to which that world view motivates you, inspires you and empowers you to embrace the other as an extension of yourself.*
>
> *The Islamic concept of peace navigates between two core values in Islam; that of compassion and justice. Whenever these two core values come into tension with each other, compassion trumps justice. In my view, a legitimate struggle for justice (jihad) has to locate itself within an ethos*

*of compassion. Without compassion, struggles for justice end up mimicking the oppressive orders against which they revolt. It is precisely here that the crisis of contemporary Muslims is located, this is where the challenge of a credible Islamic peace resides. Hence the question: How does one balance between the two critical concepts of justice and compassion in constructing a viable project of Muslim peacebuilding?*[148]

Rashied's Muslim faith commitment "to the core values of justice, "embracing the other" and compassion" puts many of us Christians to shame.

## 24. Keith Egan, T.O. Carm

KEITH J. EGAN is the Aquinas Chair in Catholic Theology Emeritus at Saint Mary's College, Notre Dame, IN, and adjunct full professor of theology at the University of Notre Dame. His doctorate is from the University of Cambridge, England. He is also the president of the North American Carmelite Institute, Washington, DC, and Fellow of the Institutum Carmelitanum in Rome, a member of the North American Carmelite Forum and past president of the College Theology Society. He has published widely on Christian and Carmelite Spirituality and has lectured throughout North America and several European countries.

Keith and his wife, Connie, are dear friends that we have lunch with to discuss the issues of the day. We were in a small Christian community, a faith sharing group called Shekan, for a number of years. More recently we both have been members of the local *Commonweal Local Community*.

I have learned much from Keith, both as a theologian and as a Carmelite. As a theologian he has impressed upon me the reality that God is Love. He is able to make his knowledge of scripture and the latest theological thought understandable in lectures, small group meetings and even in luncheon conversations. He has introduced me to the riches of Carmelite thought, especially through the poetry of St. John of the Cross.

A paragraph from the introduction to Yves Congar's, *I Believe in the Holy Spirit,* Keith made a habit of sharing with his students. It describes Keith's life as well.

> *My purpose is above all to know and to teach. I know that it is not enough to stop there. For the Christian, knowledge is there for the sake of communion and love. ... Each one of us has his gifts, his own means and his own vocation. Mine are as a Christian who prays and as a theologian who reads a great number of books and takes many notes. May I therefore be allowed to sing my own song! The Spirit is breath. The wind sings in the trees. I would like, then, to be an Aeolian Harp and let the breath of God make the strings vibrate and sing. Let me stretch and tune the strings—that will be the austere task of research. And then let the Spirit make them sing a clear and tuneful song of prayer and life! (p. X)*

Keith, like one of the great Carmelite saints, St. Therese of Lisieux, realizes "that virtue is precarious, and it is only by the thinnest of margins that the best among us are separated from the worst."[149] Keith is among the best.

# 25. John Monczunski

John Monczunski Chuck Wilber Michael Garvey

I HAVE KNOWN JOHN for over 30 years, and we have become ever closer over the last 10-15 years. We inter-acted while both of us worked at Notre Dame and we were both in the small Christian community called Shekan. We have made retreats (with Michael Garvey) at the Monastery of the Holy Cross in Chicago. More recently, he and Cheri have joined the Egan's and us for our lively lunches.

John worked for years as an editor and writer for Notre Dame Magazine. He is also a poet and finder of obscure prayers. One of John's poems has taught me that the life God has given each of us is too precious to not be embraced fully and completely.

### Memo to Self

When you taste something, savor.
When you look at something, see.
When you smell something, inhale.
When you touch something, feel.
When you hear something, listen.
None of this had to be.
Yet it is.
You did not have to be.
Yet you are.

John is one of the few people I know who are both active in the world and committed to a monk-like prayer life. He begins every day with e.e. cummings poem, "I thank you god for most this amazing day." As a meditation on gratitude it provides a good beginning for the day. Around noontime John stops for a period of centering prayer or, sometimes, his own version of the Rosary. He is thus refreshed for the afternoon's demands. He ends the day reflecting on that day using a form of the Jesuit examen prayer.

John is fueled for action by prayer. He walks the walk not just talks the talk. He delivers meals-on-wheels, pickets against injustice, and treats everyone as deserving of love and dignity. One of his poems sums up his life's journey.

### The Gospel (very) Abridged
God is love.
Jesus is love incarnate.

The Eucharist is Jesus.
What we eat becomes us.
So we are to become love.
Jesus is resurrected.

When you love, you are united to the Other.
In some sense you become the Other.
When they hurt, you cry.

Love is All Powerful.
Loves creates.
Love heals.
Love forgives.
Love redeems.

Love shows itself through actions.
Not words.

## 26. Fr. John Rausch

A GLENMARY MISSIONER for 53 years, Father John Rausch, died February 9, 2020. He was a staunch advocate for the people and environment of Appalachia and of Catholic social teaching.

Beginning in 1980, in response to the Appalachian Bishops' pastoral letter "This Land is Home to Me," John came to Notre Dame and got a master's degree in economics. He went on to establish himself as a regional worker in Appalachia doing human and economic ministry.

While at Notre Dame, John became a confidant and counselor to his classmates. He became close to my family and presided at my oldest child's wedding. John was not a great student and struggled with economic theory and the mathematics required. But he persevered and got his degree. Throughout this time his faith and commitment to justice drove him to succeed both at Notre Dame and later in his work in Appalachia.

He had a passion for educating people about the economic and environmental realities of Appalachia. To do so he turned to all manner of media and opportunities including public speaking, Appalachian pilgrimages, and almost anything else to make his point.

"Father John's mission ministry can be summarized in Pope Francis' encyclical *Laudato Si*," Father Dorsey, Glenmary's president, said. "His passion for justice, love of nature and commitment to care for creation are the hallmarks of his missionary life."

John was a talented writer as well. His writings appeared in a variety of publications, and he won 10 Catholic Press Association awards for his articles in Glenmary Challenge magazine. He was working on an autobiography for the University of Kentucky Press at the time of his death. Back in August 2019 I reviewed the chapter of his autobiography on his time at Notre Dame.

John didn't have a traditional assignment at a church but viewed all of Appalachia as his parish. He served with many institutions alongside his work in Glenmary including the Commission on Religion in Appalachia and the Appalachian Ministries Educational Resource Center. He was former director of the Catholic Committee of Appalachia and served for three years as summer faculty at the Coady Institute in Canada.

He was a wisdom figure, a champion of struggling communities in Appalachia, one of the strongest Catholic voices for the environment and an early and outspoken prophet on the climate crisis. John wrote a column for many years that was regularly featured on the Pax Christi USA website. He led retreats on Cherokee spirituality and organized pilgrimages for religious leaders and anyone else willing to come and see firsthand the economic and environmental destruction of communities in Appalachia and the resiliency of the people there who were his friends and neighbors. John received the Pax Christi USA Teacher of Peace Award in 2007 for how his life and witness spoke to the peace of Christ, care of creation, and the Church's preferential option for those who are impoverished.

I remember John as fun loving, talkative, savoring a glass of bourbon, and utterly dedicated to serving the poor, disadvantaged folks in the mountains of Appalachia. He was an exemplary witness. His last email to me was just a week before he died, reminding me that he was giving one final retreat on Cherokee spirituality before he "retired" and suggesting that I come and join him. My heart is heavy knowing that I missed that opportunity.

## 27. John Bracke, c.s.c.

FR. JAMES BRACKE, C.S.C., is the Staff Chaplain at the University of Notre Dame where he serves the staff of nearly 5,000. He entered the Congregation of Holy Cross at Notre Dame in the fall of 1970 as a collegiate freshman seminarian. He received a B.A. in Sociology in 1974 and an M.Div. in 1978. Following a transfer to the Diocese of Peoria he was ordained in 1980 at St. Mary's Cathedral. He served in 2 parishes and at the Newman Center at the University of Illinois for 9 years. In September 1988, Fr. Bracke re-incorporated into the Congregation and has since served in parochial ministry, as a chaplain to the Sisters of the Holy Cross, and as a campus minister at Notre Dame Prep in Niles, Illinois. Prior to this assignment he also served in prison ministry at Westville Correctional in Northwest Indiana.

Mary Ellen and I got to know Fr. Jim in 2000 after our son, Kenny, committed suicide. Though he had been the associate pastor at Little Flower which was our parish, we didn't really know him. But Jim was the first priest to visit us after Kenny's death. Something just clicked. His sincerity, kindness, and love gave us comfort at a very difficult time in our lives. We have remained close ever since. For years he and Reggie Weissert were our favorite dinner guests. With Reggie's death, we go to lunch with Jim, for birthdays and other celebrations.

Jim is quiet, not much of a talker, but you can't help but notice his genuineness; what I would call his holiness. I know he would demur, but I would quote to him from Leon Bloy's, *The Woman Who was Poor*: "There is only one misery...not to be saints." You can get a feel for the man from something he wrote on a Notre Dame blog, *Why We Minister:*

> *I love being a priest and have been serving God and God's People for over 38 years. I love serving the 5,000 children of God here at Notre Dame for the past 5 years. Yet, I have also had many ups and downs over the years. ... I have...been hurt by the people I have served and call family, and I have experienced depression and loneliness along the way. However, I have always been able to be open with God and share these thoughts and feelings. Sometimes God seems distant and I feel like I am in a desert just as Jesus was. I have felt temptation, but honestly, I have never felt abandoned or rejected by God. Our God is a God of love.*
>
> *The blessing of Spiritual Companions has helped me to come back to God and open my heart. ...I believe in Divine Providence and that God sends us people and events that are not just coincidence but God's way of saying, "I am with you and holding you" as if you were an infant- even if you are 66 years old.*
>
> *This is why I continue to minister.*

I thank God every day for sending me companions on the Way like Fr. Jim. That great cloud of witnesses has provided the inspiration to counter my backsliding, has shown me that hope can overcome despair, and even ordinary people like me are loved by God

# Endnotes

## Dedication

So many people were important for my life as a pilgrimage that only a few could be acknowledged in the appendices. I must mention a few more here: Ken Jameson, a colleague and dear friend and collaborator for many years; Jane Pitz, a dynamic servant of God, both as a nun and as a lay woman; Ken Milani, dear friend who carried on during the tragedies of the death of a son, the death of his wife, the death of his daughter, and his own stroke. His love, faith, and humor never wavered.

## Chapter I

[1] Joan Chittister, O.S.B., *The Rule of Benedict: Insights for the Ages*. New York, Crossroads Press, 2004.

[2] Charles K. Wilber, "Francis of Assisi," in *The SAGE Encyclopedia of World Poverty*, Second Edition, Mehmet Odekon, editor (Los Angeles, CA: SAGE Reference, 2015), Vol. 2, pp. 606-7.

[3] Charles K. Wilber, "Thomas Aquinas," in *The SAGE Encyclopedia of World Poverty*, Second Edition, Mehmet Odekon, editor (Los Angeles, CA: SAGE Reference, 2015), Vol. 1, pp. 74-6.

[4] Charles K. Wilber, "Mother Teresa," in *The SAGE Encyclopedia of World Poverty*, Second Edition, Mehmet Odekon, editor (Los Angeles, CA: SAGE Reference, 2015), Vol. 3, pp. 1071-2.

## Chapter II

[5] I cannot help wondering how Timothy handled being circumcised as an adult at the demand of St. Paul because everyone knew his father was a Greek. See Acts 16: 1-10.

[6] See Appendix 2.

[7] See Appendix 5.

[8] See Appendix 1.

## Chapter III

[9] See Appendix 3.

[10] See Appendix 6.

[11] See Appendix 8.

[12] Charles K. Wilber. *Catholics Spending and Acting Justly*. Notre Dame, IN: Ave Maria Press, 2011, pp. 39-48.

[13] Michael Kirwan, "Hospitality and Mutual Trust," *The Catholic Worker*. Cited in Eugene A. Thalman, M.M., *Thou Shalt Think and Do! Adventures with the Social Teachings of the Catholic Church*, Volume One, Hong Kong: Asian Center for the Progress of Peoples, 2004).

[14] See http://smallchristiancommunities.org/; https://www.cfm.org/; Charles K. Wilber, *Catholics Spending and Acting Justly* (Ave Maria Press, 2011).

[15] References to Papal documents will be included in the text. References to other sources will be included in the end notes.

[16] In most CST documents the paragraphs are numbered. Thus, the numbers in brackets refer to paragraphs.

[17]See Charles K. Wilber. *Beyond Reaganomics: A Further Inquiry into the Poverty of Economics* (University of Notre Dame Press, 1990), with Kenneth P. Jameson.

[18]See Appendix 3.

[19]See Appendix 4.

[20]See Jeffrey M. Burns, *Disturbing the Peace: A History of the Christian Family Movement*, 1949-1974. University of Notre Dame Press, 1999. See Appendix 7.

[21]Rose Marciano Lucy. *Roots and Wings: Deamers and Doers of the Christian Family Movement*. San Jose, CA: Resource Publications, Inc, 1987.

[22]Burns, pp. 42-43, 73-76, 86. See Appendix 9.

[23]Bob Ghelardi. *We are Church: The Life and Times of Louis J. Putz, c.s.c., Prophet, Servant and Visionary.* Salem, NH: GOAL/OPC, 2006. See Appendix 6.

[24]Henri Nouwen. Forword to *Roots and Wings*, p. vii.

## Chapter IV

[25]See Appendix 10.

[26]He started work as a priest in an Irish and Puerto Rican parish in New York, popularizing the church through close contact with the Latino community and respect for their traditions. He applied these same methods on a larger scale when, in 1956, he was appointed vice-rector of the Catholic University of Puerto Rico, and later, in 1961, as founder of the Centro Intercultural de Doc umentación (CIDOC) at Cuernavaca in Mexico, a broad-based research center which offered courses and briefings for missionaries arriving from North America. For further information on Illich, see https://www.theguardian.com/news/2002/dec/09/guardianobituaries.highereducation.

## Chapter V

[27]See Appendix 12.

[28]See Appendix 11.

[29]Dorothy often quoted from Fyodor Dostoevsky's *The Brothers Karamazov*, where Fr. Zosima says, "Love in Action is a harsh and dreadful thing compared to love in dreams."

[30]At that time Trinity was a college for well-off, smart women. Patty Crowley graduated from there some years earlier. I had many fine students. A friend of one of my students, who I didn't get to teach, went on to considerable fame-Nancy D'Alesandro-Pelosi.

[31]Many tears later, Louie now married with a son, decided to get a DNA test from Ancestry.com. It showed he is 64 percent Italian. Obviously, St. Ann's was wrong.

[32]Ibid.

## Chapter VI

[33]See F. Knox, "The Doctrine of Consumer Sovereignty," *Review of Social Economy*, Vol. 18, No. 2 (1960), pp. 138-149.

[34]Adam Smith (1776). *An inquiry into the nature and causes of the wealth of nations*, ed. W. B. Todd, Vol. 2 of *The Glasgow edition of the works and correspondences of Adam Smith*, general editors, D. D. Raphael and A. Skinner, Oxford: Clarendon Press, 1976.

[35]Adam Smith (1789). *The theory of moral sentiments*, ed. D. D. Raphael and A. L. Macfie, Vol. 1 of *The Glasgow edition of the works and correspondences of Adam Smith*, general editors, D. D. Raphael and A. Skinner, Oxford: Clarendon Press, 1976.

[36]Jerry Evensky. *"Ethics and the Invisible Hand." Journal of Economic Perspectives*, 7:2 (Spring 1993), pp. 197-205.

[37]Smith, *Theory of Moral Sentiments*, 1789, p. 190.

[38]Ibid., p. 244.

[39]Pope Francis, *Laudato Si*, para. 109, 123.

[40]My dissertation was published by the University of North Carolina Press in 1969 and republished in a new series in 2017.

[41]See *The Political Economy of Development and Underdevelopment: A Book of Readings* (Random House, 1973; 2nd edition, 1979; 3rd edition, 1983; 4th edition, 1988; McGraw-Hill: 5th edition, 1992; 6th edition, 1996). The second edition translated into Chinese and published by Chinese Social Science Publishing House, 1984; *Growth with Equity: Essays on Economic Development* (Paulist Press,1979). with Mary Evelyn Jegen (eds.); *Directions in Economic Development* (University of Notre Dame Press, 1979). with Kenneth P. Jameson (eds); *Religious Values and Development* (Pergamon Press, 1980), with Kenneth P. Jameson (eds); *Socialist Models of Development* (Pergamon Press, 1982), with Kenneth P. Jameson (eds); *New Directions in Development Ethics: Essays in Honor of Denis Goulet* (University of Notre Dame Press, 2010), with Amitava Krishna Dutt (eds.).

[42]The term was coined in 1989 by John Williamson, of the Institute for International Economics, to describe the conventional wisdom at the U.S. Treasury Department, the World Bank, and the International Monetary Fund on policy reforms that would aid development in Latin America. Over time the term took hold in public debate, where the Washington Consensus became synonymous with market fundamentalism, globally applied. A short-hand term was "get your prices right."

[43]Denis died in 2006 from leukemia. In his honor a festschrift was published. See Charles K. Wilber and Amitava Krishna Dutt (eds). *New Directions in Development Ethics: Essays in Honor of Denis Goulet* (University of Notre Dame Press, 2010). Also see Appendix 14 at the end of this book.

[44]Denis Goulet. *The Cruel Choice: A New Concept in the Theory of Development*, New York: Atheneum 1971 and Goulet, Denis. 'Development Experts: The One-Eyed Giants,' *World Development*, 8:7/8, (July/August 1980), 481-489.

[45]Audience with the participants in the Convention organized by the Dicastery for Promoting Integral Human Development on the fiftieth anniversary of "Populorum Progressio" (2018)

[46]Charles Dickens, *Hard Times*, Book 1, Chapter 2.

[47]Op. cit., Book 2, Chapter 12.

[48]Op. cit., Book 3, Chapter 1

[49]See Isaiah Berlin. "The Hedgehog and the Fox: An Essay of Tolstoy's View of History." In H. Hardy (Ed.) *Russian Thinkers*. Princeton, NJ: Princeton University Press, 2013.

[50]Gary Saul Morson and Morton Schapiro. *Cents and Sensibility: What Economics Can Learn from the Humanities*. Princeton, NJ: Princeton University Press, 2017. Cited by Jeffrey R. Bloem in a review in *Faith & Economics*, No. 71, Spring 2018, p.75.

[51]Cited in John Lanchester, "Can Economists and Humanists Ever be Friends?" *The New Yorker* (July 16, 2018), https://www.newyorker.com/magazine/2018/07/23/can-economists-and-humanists-ever-be-friends. Review of Morson and Schapiro.

[52]Ibid.

[53] The common good is defined by Dempsey (pp. 272-273) as the fulfillment of the needs of human beings which arise from their living together, as in the case of public health, instead of each one living alone. Two characteristics set these needs off: (1) they are common to all, and (2) they can be met only through the united efforts of all members of the community acting together. The fulfillment of these

common needs depends critically on each person contributing to the community because the community by itself has nothing to contribute to its members apart from what its various members contribute to it (Dempsey, pp. 219-220). Thus, is the common good dependent on contributive justice.

[54] Reason discovers truth from direct, personal experience; faith accepts truth on the word of another.

[55] Based on Edward O'Boyle. "Requiem for Homo Economicus," *Markets and Morality*, volume 10, number 2, 2007, pp. 321-338.

[56] P. Danner. *The Economic Person*, Rowman and Littlefield Publishers, London 2002.

[57] However, of late, O'Boyle has been using instead "the acting person" and "the person in action." See his article in *Markets and Morality*, 2007. The reasons are to underscore the difference between the individual and the person and to highlight acting as critical to being more. Also see Danner's *The Economic Person*.

[58] Amitava Krishna Dutt and Charles K. Wilber. *Economics and Ethics: An Introduction*, Palgrave Press, New York and London 2010. Revised paperback edition, 2013.

[59] See Charles K. Wilber and Amitava Krishna Dutt. *New Directions in Development Ethics: Essays in Honor of Denis Goulet* (University of Notre Dame Press, 2010).

[60] Denis Goulet. "Inequalities in the light of globalization," in Louis Sabourin, ed., *Globalisation and Inequalities*, Vatican City: Pontifical Academy of Social Sciences, 2002, 3-29.

[61] Denis Goulet. *Development Ethics at Work: Explorations 1960-2002*, Routledge, New York 2006.

[62] Charles K. Wilber, "Sustainable Development, Consumerism, & Catholic Social Thought." *In Looking Beyond the Individualism & Homo Economicus of Neoclassical Economics*, ed. Edward J. O'Boyle, Milwaukee, WI: Marquette University Press, 2011,129-43.

[63] Denis Goulet. "On Culture, Religion, and Development," *Reclaiming Democracy*, (ed.) Marguerite Mendell, Montreal & Kingston, London, Ithaca: McGill-Queen's University Press, 2005, 21-32.

[64] Wilber, "Sustainable Development, Consumerism, & Catholic Social Thought" and Goulet. *Development Ethics at Work*.

[65] Quoted from Stanley Hauerwas, David Burrell, and Richard Bondi, *Truthfulness and Tragedy: A Further Investigation in Christian Ethics*, Notre Dame, IN: University of Notre Dame Press, 1977.

[66] See Appendix 13.

[67] James H. Weaver, "*Globalization with a Human Face.*" Paper delivered to the Association for Social Economics, ASSA Convention, 2004, San Diego, CA.

# Chapter VII

[68] David Brooks, "The Rise of the Haphazard Self," *New York Times*, May 14, 2019.

[69] Ibid.

[70] Peter Berger, "In Praise of Particularity: The Concept of Mediating Structures," published in *The Review of Politics* (July, 1976) and in Walter Nicgorski and Ronald Weber (eds.), *An Almost Chosen People* (Notre Dame, Ind.: University of Notre Dame Press, 1976).

[71] Elizabeth Warren and Amelia Warren Tyagi. *The Two-Income Trap: Why Middle-Class Parents are (Still) Going Broke*. Basic Books, Revised, updated edition, 2016.

[72]Anne Case and Angus Deaton. *Deaths of Despair and the Future of Capitalism.* Princeton: Princeton University Press, 2020, 312pp.

[73]Pope John Paul II, *Familiaris Consortio* (Washington, D.C.: United States Catholic Conference, 1981), p. 43.

[74]See Proceedings of the Latin American Bishops Conference, Puebla, Mexico (Notre Dame, Ind.: CCUM, 1979).

[75]"Decree on the Apostolate of the Laity," *The Documents of Vatican II* (New York: Guild Press, 1966), p. 503.

[76]"Toward the Synod of 1980," p. 127.

[77]*Familiaris Consortio*, pp. 42, 45.

[78]Rosemary Haughton, "Testimony on the Family," Liberty and Justice for All: Atlanta Hearing (National Conference of Catholic Bishops, Committee for the Bicentennial, August 9, 1975), p. 67.

[79]One of our children bought Mary Ellen for her birthday a dish towel that said "OMG, my mother was right every time."

[80]"Decree on the Apostolate of the Laity," p. 518.

[81]Eugene S. Geissler, "Our Children Our Greatest Teachers," in *Marriage Among Christians* ed. James T. Burtchaell, C.S.C. (Notre Dame, Ind.: Ave Maria Press, 1977), pp. 58, 61 62.

[82]See http://smallchristiancommunities.org/; https://www.cfm.org/; Charles K. Wilber, *Catholics Spending and Acting Justly* (Ave Maria Press, 2011).

[83]See Appendix 13.

[84]See Appendix 14.

[85]See Appendix 15.

# Chapter VIII

[86]See Appendix 20.

[87]See Charles K. Wilber and Kenneth P. Jameson. *An Inquiry into the Poverty of Economics* (University of Notre Dame Press, 1983), 294 pages.

[88]C. Jencks and D. Riesman, *The Academic Revolution* (1968).

[89]Hamid Bouchikhi and John Kimberly, "How identity and power shape an organization's responses to isomorphic pressures: The battle over the soul of economics at the University of Notre Dame," p.11.

[90]Under the leadership of Fr. John Jenkins, c.s.c., , the university has done much more to attract Catholic academics who see their faith being important for their professional work. They have created research institutes and endowed chairs designed to attract just such people.

[91]The recent increase in categories of faculty has been a positive move. There are now Teaching Professors, Professors of the Practice, et al; each with their own duties.

[92]See "Empirical Verification and Theory Selection: The Keynesian-Monetarist Debate," *Journal of Economic Issues*, Vol. XIII, No. 4 (December 1979), pp. 973-982.

[93]David Colander, *The Making of an Economist, Redux* (Princeton University Press, 2007).

[94]Ibid., p.2.

[95]Smith, *Theory of Moral Sentiments*, 1789, p. 244.

[96]Evensky, Jerry. "Ethics and the Invisible Hand." *Journal of Economic Perspectives*, 7:2 (Spring 1993), pp. 197-205.

[97]See Charles K. Wilber (ed.), *Economics, Ethics and Public Policy* (Rowman & Littlefield, 1998). Also published on Android Market. See https://market.android.com/details?id=book-y-N9VNpXjawC&feature=null-Charles+K.+Wilber; and Amitava Krishna Dutt and Charles K. Wilber. *Economics and Ethics.*

*An Introduction* (Palgrave Press, 2010), with Revised paperback edition, 2013.

[98]Cited in John Lanchester, "Can Economists and Humanists Ever be Friends?" *The New Yorker* (July 16, 2018), https://www.newyorker.com/magazine/2018/07/23/can-economists-and-humanists-ever-be-friends. Review of Morson and Schapiro.

[99]While attending my granddaughter's graduation from the Massachusetts Institute of Technology (MIT), they announced that among the faculty there were 45 Nobel Prize winners. Notre Dame would be overjoyed with one.

[100]U.S. Catholic Bishops. *Economic Justice for All: Pastoral Letter on Catholic Social Teaching and the U.S. Economy.* U.S. National Catholic Conference of Bishops: Washington, D.C., November 18, 1986. Reprinted in *Catholic Social Thought: The Documentary Heritage*, ed. David J. O'Brien and Thomas A. Shannon, 572-680. Maryknoll, New York: Orbis Books, 1992.

[101]This office was funded for five years and its success was spotty at best.

[102]See Appendix 16.

[103]See Appendix 17.

[104]I need to admit that the preceding paragraphs have been liberally paraphrased from Michael's fund-raising letters.

[105]See Appendix 21.

[106]See Appendix 18.

[107]See Appendix 19.

[108]See his *God, Country, Notre Dame: The Autobiography of Theodore M. Hesburgh.* University of Notre Dame Press, 1999.

[109]The Hesburgh Papers, 1979.

[110]See Appendix 24.

[111]See Appendix 23.

# Chapter IX

[112]Michael J. Baxter, "Notes on Catholic Americanism and Catholic Radical ism: Toward a Counter-Tradition of Catholic Social Ethics," in *American Catholic Traditions: Resources for Renewal*, eds. Sandra Yowm Mize and William L. Portier (Maryknoll, NY: Orbis Books, 1997), pp. 53-71.

[113]This view has been ridiculed by Bernard Lonergan as "the principle of the empty head." Quoted in Baxter 1995, p. 285.

[114]Michael J. Baxter and Frederick C. Bauerschmidt, "*Eruditio* without *religio*?: The dilemma of Catholics in the academy," *Communio* 22 (Summer 1995), p. 287.

[115]One of my graduate students in the early 1980s, Fr. John Rausch, always insisted we needed to see the actual people that lay behind the abstract terms, worker, consumer, investor. See Appendix 26.

[116]Mother Teresa always said that love and dignity are what are most needed.

[117]See Appendix 11.

[118]Brigid O'Shea Merriman, O.S.F. *Searching for Christ: The Spirituality of Dorothy Day*. Notre Dame: University of Notre Dame Press, 1994.

[119]I maintain my relationship when I cannot get to Chicago through the website https://chicagomonk.org/.

[120]Cyprian Smith, Osb. *The Path of Life*. Gracewing Publishing, 1995.

[121]See Appendix 25.

[122]Don Talafous, OSB, "Were and Now and Hereafter," *Give Us this Day*. November 26, 2019, pp.278-9.

[123]Kenneth E. Boulding, *Beyond Economics* (Ann Arbor: University of Michigan Press, 1968.)

# Appendices

[124]*ACT: A Quarterly of Adult Catholic Action*, v. 14, no. 3 (November 1960).

[125]Bob Ghelardi. *You Are Church! The Life and Times of Louis J. Putz, C.S.C., Prophet, Servant and Visionary*. Salem, NH: Goal QPC, 2006, p. v.

[126]Ibid, p. 46.

[127]See Robert J. McClory, "Patty Crowley, giant of Catholic laity, dies at 92," *National Catholic Reporter*, December 9, 2005.

[128]Ibid.

[129]Ibid.

[130]Ibid.

[131]Rose Marciano Lucey. *Roots and Wings: Dreamers and Doers of the Christian Family Movement*. San Jose, CA: Resource Publications, Inc, 1987, p.58.

[132]See https://womenintheology.org/2012/02/23/women-speak-about-natural-family-planning-patty-crowleys-speech-to-the-papal-birth-control-commission-2/

[133]Robert McClory. *Turning Point: The Inside Story of the Papal Birth Control Commission, and How Humanae Vitae Changed the Life of Patty Crowley and the Future of the Church*. New York: Crossroad, 1995, p. 1.

[134]McClory, *Turning Point*.

[135]Ibid.

[136]See Mario Carota, *Actipan*. www.amigosanonymous.org/actipan.html.

[137]Donald P. McNeill, Douglas A. Morrison, Henri J.M. Nouwen, *Compassion: A Reflection on the Christian Life*. Doubleday & Co.: New York, 1982.

[138]https://news.nd.edu/news/in-memoriam-rev-donald-p-mcneill-csc-founding-director-of-notre-dames-center-for-social-concerns/

[139]Rosalie Riegle Troester (ed), *Voices from the Catholic Worker* "The Logic of Grace: Davenport, Iowa," pp. 357-69.

[140]Ibid, p. 362.

[141]Ibid, p. 360.

[142]https://northcoastview.blogspot.com/2014/11/an-amazing-one-woman-play-on-dorothy.html

[143]Michael Garvey. *Confessions of a Catholic Worker*. Notre Dame: Ave Maria Press, 1978.

[144]Kerry Walters, https://smile.amazon.com/Confessions-Catholic-Worker-Michael-Garvey/dp/0883470918/ref=sr_1_1?keywords=Confessions+of+a+Catholic+Worker&qid=1571595871&sr=8-1

[145]See, for example, *Walking with God in a Fragile World, The Spirit of Notre Dame, The Times of My Life, The Cub Fan's Guide to Life*.

[146]A quote from Jim's book, *The Times of My Life:* "…Jill and I decided we needed to go our separate ways. We were both sad about it. In the interest of preserving our deep friendship and continuing to nurture our two minor children, we parted amicably, even using the same lawyer." P. 185.

[147]Carol Schaal, *"There are Children Here,"* Notre Dame Magazine, Summer 2001.

[148]https://www.beyondintractability.org/profile/a-rashied-omar

[149]Michael Casey, o.c.s.o., "Tribal Standards," *Give Us this Day*, October 1, 2019.